Great Taste ~ Low Fat

ITALIAN COOKING

ALEXANDRIA, VIRGINIA

TABLE OF CONTENTS

Linguine with Fresh Clams in Red Sauce

page 54

Appetizers

Pasta

Poultry, Meat & Seafood

Steak with Balsamic Sauce and Mushrooms

~

page 90

Side Dishes

Desserts

~

INTRODUCTION

Our mission at Great Taste-Low Fat is to take the work and worry out of everyday low-fat cooking; to provide delicious, fresh, and filling recipes for family and friends; to use quick, streamlined methods and available ingredients; and, within every recipe, to keep the percentage of calories from fat under 30 percent.

When asked to name their favorite cuisine, most Americans will say "Italian"—and Italian has been number one for a long time. It all began about a century ago, with the enormous wave of Italian immigration: Some of the new residents opened restaurants, popularizing the cuisine of their homeland and forever enlivening the American food scene. Such delights as steaming pasta with robust sauces and delicately seasoned meats were all enthusiastically presented as an edible adventure rather than a quick route to a full belly.

A HEALTHY HERITAGE

The Italians have enjoyed a hearty-but-healthful cooking style for centuries, centering their meals around low-fat carbohydrates such as pasta, rice, and beans, and partnering these staples with a wide variety of vegetables, with meat, poultry, seafood, and robust cheeses served as flavor accents. Italian cooks are masters at seasoning, making brilliant use of herbs, garlic, dried mushrooms, anchovies, wine vinegar, and the like. However, as their cuisine took root amidst America's bounty, something changed: Meat and cheese came to the fore while vegetables, grains, and legumes dwindled into insignificance. An Italian restaurant meal might start with fried mozzarella, proceed to a plate-dwarfing slab of veal parmi-

giana, and conclude with a hefty slice of cheesecake. We thought it was time to turn back the clock to a healthier era in Italian cooking.

BACK TO BASICS

Chef Sandra Gluck, who loves Italian food, happily accepted the challenge of updating the classics and creating new dishes with traditional ingredients. In her travels to Italy, Sandra discovered that "there's not just one Italian cuisine, but many. Northern and Southern Italian food can be quite different." The humble tomato-based dishes of Sicily are worlds apart from the subtle, sophisticated cooking of Milan. Foods Sandra enjoyed in Italy gave rise to some of the recipes in this book: A sublimely rich *panna cotta* (cream custard) inspired the light but luscious Latte Cotta you'll find in the desserts chapter. As Italian cooks have always done, Sandra plans her menus according to what's in season and looks best at the market. She's also an expert on the key ingredients that make Italian food special (see "Secrets of Italian Cooking"), and always keeps them on hand.

THROUGH THE MENU

An Italian meal often begins with a selection of *antipasti*—tasty little bites to whet the appetite—and we've kept them light: Our bruschetta, marinated mushrooms, and focaccia all use less olive oil than standard recipes. In Italy, pastas are often *primi piatti* (first courses), but our hearty low-fat pastas are meant to be main dishes. Dig into our Fettuccine with Shrimp and Lemon Cream Sauce guilt free, knowing that low-fat milk and cornstarch (rather than cream) thicken the sauce. Our rich-tasting Straw and Hay with Pesto alla Genovese also boasts a secret ingredient: reduced-fat cream cheese. The other main dishes are delectable but light, made with carefully chosen cuts of beef and pork, skinless chicken and game hens, as well as succulent swordfish, shrimp, and other seafood. Lavish use of fresh herbs, a splash of balsamic vinegar, or an occasional touch of savory prosciutto lifts these dishes out of the ordinary. The *contorni*—side dishes—reflect the Italian love of vegetables, from artichokes to zucchini. Try Polenta with Tomato-Mushroom Sauce, fragrant with Gorgonzola and rosemary, as a change from mashed potatoes. In true Italian fashion, our desserts focus on fruit, but there are some special occasion indulgences as well, including an ice-cream-like *semifreddo* and Ricotta Cheesecake.

We think you'll appreciate this timely return to simple, satisfying Italian food that honors your healthy instincts as well as your palate.

CONTRIBUTING EDITORS

Sandra Rose Gluck, a New York City chef, has years of experience creating delicious low-fat recipes that are quick to prepare. Her secret for satisfying results is to always aim for great taste and variety. By combining readily available, fresh ingredients with simple cooking techniques, Sandra has created the perfect recipes for today's busy lifestyles.

Grace Young has been the director of a major test kitchen specializing in low-fat and health-related cookbooks for over 12 years. Grace oversees the development, taste testing, and nutritional analysis of every recipe in Great Taste-Low Fat. Her goal is simple: take the work and worry out of low-fat cooking so that you can enjoy delicious, healthy meals every day.

Kate Slate has been a food editor for almost 20 years, and has published thousands of recipes in cookbooks and magazines. As the Editorial Director of Great Taste-Low Fat, Kate combined simple, easy to follow directions with practical low-fat cooking tips. The result is guaranteed to make your low-fat cooking as rewarding and fun as it is foolproof.

NUTRITION

Every recipe in *Great Taste-Low Fat* provides per-serving values for the nutrients listed in the chart at right. The daily intakes listed in the chart are based on those recommended by the USDA and presume a nonsedentary lifestyle. The nutritional emphasis in this book is not only on controlling calories, but on reducing total fat grams. Research has shown that dietary fat metabolizes more easily into body fat than do carbohydrates and protein. In order to control the amount of fat in a given recipe and in your diet in general, no more than 30 percent of the calories should come from fat.

Nutrient	Women	Men
Fat	<65 g	<80 g
Calories	2000	2500
Saturated fat	<20 g	<25 g
Carbohydrate	300 g	375 g
Protein	50 g	65 g
Cholesterol	<300 mg	<300 mg
Sodium	<2400 mg	<2400 mg

These recommended daily intakes are averages used by the Food and Drug Administration and are consistent with the labeling on all food products. Although the values for cholesterol and sodium are the same for all adults, the other intake values vary depending on gender, ideal weight, and activity level. Check with a physician or nutritionist for your own daily intake values.

SECRETS OF LOW-FAT ITALIAN COOKING

LOW-FAT ITALIAN COOKING

Italian food has become so universally popular in this country that the phrase "as American as pizza pie" makes perfect sense. At the heart of this cuisine are fine fresh ingredients and robust seasonings, making it a natural for adaptation to low-fat cooking. Just a few commonsense adjustments make Italian dishes low in fat. Sometimes we modify the ingredients. For instance, although olive oil is an indispensable component of the Italian pantry, we cut the quantities way down. Northern Italian recipes often call for butter; we substitute oil where possible to reduce saturated fat. Happily, some of Italy's great cheeses are now made in low-fat forms; when authenticity demands a full-fat cheese such as Gorgonzola, we use it sparingly.

Cooking techniques can also be altered to reduce fat. Our Chicken Milanese, for example, is breaded, drizzled with oil, and then baked; the result is savory, crisp-crusted chicken with just a fraction of the fat found in the classic sautéed version.

Pasta, that staple of the Italian diet, is naturally low in fat. When tossed with a flavorful low-fat sauce, pasta makes a satisfying meal. Our generous portions reflect the American preference for pasta as a main dish, rather than a first course.

ITALIAN FLAVOR ENHANCERS

Many of the ingredients in Italian cooking are powerhouses of flavor. Some, like herbs and sun-dried tomatoes, are fat free; the richer ones, such as prosciutto, are so intensely flavored that a small amount has a big impact. It's worth a trip to your local Italian delicatessen or gourmet grocer to have all of the following ingredients on hand.

• Garlic, herbs, and spices: There's no substitute for fresh garlic; mince it with a knife or crush it in a press, as you prefer. Dried oregano, sage, and rosemary are favorite herbs in the Italian kitchen; fiery red pepper flakes and licorice-flavored fennel seeds are also important seasonings. Herbs and spices don't keep forever: Replace them if they're not fragrant when rubbed between your fingers.

• Greens. Flat-leaf Italian parsley is more flavorful than curly parsley; fragrant fresh basil, now available the year round, is a must for authentic pesto. Arugula, a leafy green vegetable, adds a unique peppery bite to salads. Watercress, which has a similar tart-bitter taste, can be substituted.

• Aged cheeses. You don't have to pile on the cheese for a great Italian meal: Only small amounts of assertive well-aged Parmigiano-Reggiano (Italy's finest Parmesan), Romano (sharper and saltier than Parmesan), and pungent green-veined Gorgonzola are needed to add deep, rich cheese flavor to low-fat dishes. For the best flavor, buy Parmesan and Romano in a chunk to grate as needed. Pre-grated cheese just can't compare.

• Dried mushrooms. Reconstituted in water or broth, these add a deep, "meaty" flavor to sauces and soups. Italian porcini are excellent, but other dried mushrooms, from the generic supermarket variety to shiitake, are fine for our recipes.

• Meats and fish. Pancetta is a salt-and-spice-cured, unsmoked bacon; salt-cured prosciutto is an air-dried ham. Use slivers of these intensely flavored meats to season sauces without adding a lot of fat. Anchovies and anchovy paste, used judiciously, add a savory quality—not a fishy flavor.

• Olives, oil, and vinegar. Brine-cured black olives have a robust bouquet. Save fine-flavored extra-virgin olive oil for salad dressings and other uncooked foods, where its flavor can shine. Rich-tasting balsamic vinegar is mild, so you need less oil in dressings; it's also wonderful as a seasoning.

• Tomatoes. Sun-dried tomatoes and tomato paste represent this quintessential Italian ingredient in its most concentrated forms. For low-fat meals, buy sun-dried tomatoes that are not packed in oil.

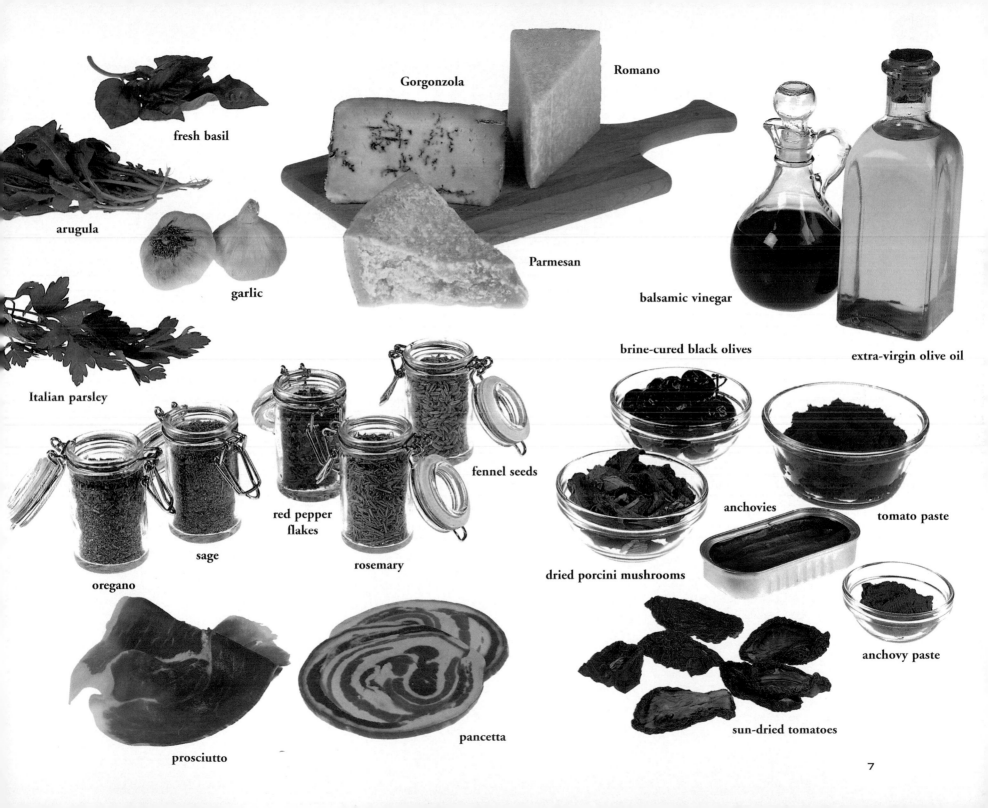

fresh basil

Gorgonzola

Romano

arugula

garlic

Parmesan

balsamic vinegar

brine-cured black olives

extra-virgin olive oil

Italian parsley

fennel seeds

anchovies

tomato paste

red pepper
flakes

sage

rosemary

dried porcini mushrooms

oregano

anchovy paste

prosciutto

pancetta

sun-dried tomatoes

7

Italian Olive Oil

Olive oil is fundamental to Italian cooking. In earlier times, only southern Italians cooked with olive oil (northerners favored butter), but this ingredient is now appreciated throughout the country. The variety of olives and the climate and soil in which they were grown affect the quality and flavor of the oil; sample different brands and types until you find one you like. The color of olive oil ranges from pale gold to deep green, but color is not an indication of quality. Instead, go by the grade you'll find on the label: This designates the level of acidity in the oil. Extra-virgin olive oil is the highest quality oil with the least acid; cold-pressed extra-virgin oil is processed without heat or further refinement. The fruity flavor of extra-virgin oil doesn't stand up well to heat and is best used in cold dishes or added after cooking. Other oils are graded (in descending order of quality) as superfine virgin, fine virgin, virgin, and pure. Virgin oil is excellent for cooking.

Italian Pastas, Rice, and Beans

Although many cuisines feature noodles in various forms, *pasta* is quintessentially Italian. It is made in a wide array of shapes and sizes, from diminutive ditalini (little thimbles) used in soups to substantial rigatoni suited to chunky sauces to corkscrew fusilli that go well with a thick tomato *ragù*. The best pastas are made from semolina flour, which is ground from durum wheat. If not overcooked, good pasta remains slightly firm (al dente). Beans, chickpeas, and lentils, excellent low-fat protein sources, can be combined with pasta for a satisfying, nutritious meal; they also make great side dishes and salads. Canned beans and chick-peas are ready to use after rinsing; dried lentils cook quickly. Arborio rice is one of a select few varieties favored for the famed dish, *risotto*. Plump grains of arborio rice remain firm at the center while the outer portion of the rice "melts" into a creamy sauce.

Fresh Cheeses

Mozzarella and ricotta are familiar fresh, or unripened, Italian cheeses. Because they are not aged, fresh cheeses are mild in flavor. Mozzarella is made by the "drawn-curd" process, in which the curds are kneaded and stretched to develop the characteric stringiness of melted mozzarella. Mozzarella comes plain and smoked—the latter a surprisingly savory contrast to plain mozzarella's milky mildness. Mozzarella was originally made from water-buffalo milk, but it is now commonly made from cow's milk. Part-skim mozzarella doesn't melt quite as smoothly as the whole-milk version, but it can make a big difference in the fat content of a hearty lasagna or pizza. Ricotta bears some resemblance to cottage cheese, but it is moister and somewhat grainy in texture, and does not have distinct curds; it is used both in pasta dishes and desserts. Traditionally, ricotta was made from the whey (liquid) that was a by-product of manufacturing other cheeses, such as mozzarella. However, in this country most ricotta is made from a combination of whey and whole or skim milk. We've used part-skim ricotta in our recipes. Unsalted, small curd low-fat cottage cheese can be substituted for ricotta, if necessary.

APPETIZERS

1

O_n the Italian island of Sicily, everyday food tends to be humble yet intensely flavorful, thanks in part to the tomatoes and herbs that thrive under Sicily's hot sun. This pizza—boasting a tomato sauce zesty with anchovies and oregano, a topping of onions, olives, and a sprinkling of robust Romano cheese—is no exception.

Sicilian Pizza

SERVES: 4
WORKING TIME: 35 MINUTES
TOTAL TIME: 45 MINUTES

2 teaspoons yellow cornmeal

1½ cups flour

5 tablespoons grated Romano or Parmesan cheese

2 teaspoons baking powder

½ teaspoon baking soda

¼ teaspoon salt

¾ cup low-fat (1.5%) buttermilk

2 teaspoons olive oil

1 teaspoon grated lemon zest

8-ounce can no-salt-added tomato sauce

2 anchovy fillets, finely chopped, or 2 teaspoons anchovy paste

¾ teaspoon dried oregano

½ cup chopped fresh parsley

1 onion, cut into thin rings

2 tablespoons chopped Calamata or other brine-cured black olives

1. Preheat the oven to 450°. Spray a 12-inch pizza pan with nonstick cooking spray and sprinkle with the cornmeal.

2. In a large bowl, combine the flour, 2 tablespoons of the Romano, the baking powder, baking soda, and salt. Make a well in the center of the flour mixture and add the buttermilk, oil, and lemon zest to the center. Stir the dry ingredients into the wet until just combined. Do not overmix.

3. Form the dough into a loose ball and gently roll it out on a lightly floured surface to an 8-inch round (see tip; top photo). Transfer the dough to the pizza pan and pat out to an 11-inch round (middle photo). In a small bowl, combine the tomato sauce, anchovies, and oregano. Spoon the sauce onto the dough. Sprinkle with the parsley, onion rings, the remaining 3 tablespoons Romano, and the olives (bottom photo).

4. Bake for 15 minutes, or until the crust is browned on the bottom. Let stand 5 minutes before cutting into wedges and serving.

Helpful hint: You can use a large baking sheet in place of the pizza pan if you like—just press the dough into a 12 x 8-inch rectangle.

FAT: 7G/21%
CALORIES: 307
SATURATED FAT: 1G
CARBOHYDRATE: 50G
PROTEIN: 11G
CHOLESTEROL: 10MG
SODIUM: 801MG

Tomato Bruschetta

SERVES: 4
WORKING TIME: 25 MINUTES
TOTAL TIME: 25 MINUTES

In its most basic form, bruschetta consists of slabs of coarse bread toasted over coals and drizzled generously with olive oil. In our version, we rub the bread with garlic and top it with basil and tomatoes, eliminating the need for so much oil—there's just one teaspoon of it in the tomato mixture.

4 ounces Italian bread, cut into 8 slices

2 cloves garlic, peeled

2 large tomatoes, diced

¼ cup chopped fresh basil

1 teaspoon extra-virgin olive oil

½ teaspoon salt

¼ teaspoon freshly ground black pepper

1. In a toaster oven or under the broiler, toast the bread on both sides. Cut 1 clove of garlic in half and rub both sides of the toast with it. Set aside.

2. In a small pot of boiling water, cook the remaining garlic clove for 2 minutes to blanch. Transfer the garlic to a cutting board and mince. In a medium bowl, combine the tomatoes, basil, oil, salt, pepper, and the minced garlic.

3. Arrange the toast on a plater. Dividing evenly, spoon the tomato mixture over the toast and serve.

Helpful hints: If the tomatoes you're using seem watery, halve them crosswise and squeeze out some of the juice before dicing them. Even with meaty tomatoes, the topping will tend to soak into and soften the toast, so don't make the bruschetta until right before you are ready to serve it.

FAT: 2G/17%
CALORIES: 108
SATURATED FAT: .5G
CARBOHYDRATE: 19G
PROTEIN: 3G
CHOLESTEROL: 0MG
SODIUM: 446MG

CLAMS WITH WHITE WINE AND GARLIC

SERVES: 4
WORKING TIME: 25 MINUTES
TOTAL TIME: 25 MINUTES

4 ounces Italian bread, cut into 8 slices

1 clove garlic, halved, plus 3 cloves garlic, minced

2 teaspoons olive oil

3 shallots, finely chopped, or ⅓ cup chopped scallions

¾ cup dry white wine

½ teaspoon dried oregano

¼ teaspoon red pepper flakes

24 littleneck clams

2 tablespoons chopped fresh parsley

1. In a toaster oven or under the broiler, toast the bread on both sides. Rub both sides of the toast with the cut garlic.

2. In a large nonstick skillet, heat the oil until hot but not smoking over medium heat. Add the shallots and minced garlic and cook, stirring frequently, until the shallots are softened, about 2 minutes. Add the wine, oregano, and red pepper flakes. Bring to a boil and cook for 1 minute.

3. Add the clams to the skillet, cover, and cook just until the clams open up, about 4 minutes. With a slotted spoon, transfer the clams to 4 shallow soup bowls, discarding any clams that have not opened. Stir the parsley into the skillet and spoon the sauce over the clams. Place 2 slices of garlic toast in each bowl and serve.

Helpful hint: When buying clams, be sure that the shells are tightly closed. If any are slightly open, tap them with your fingertip: They should snap shut. Use live clams within a day of buying them.

FAT: 4G/18%
CALORIES: 200
SATURATED FAT: .6G
CARBOHYDRATE: 19G
PROTEIN: 14G
CHOLESTEROL: 29MG
SODIUM: 217MG

The northern coastal region of Liguria is home to disarmingly simple shellfish preparations like this one (when seafood is impeccably fresh, it doesn't need much in the way of dressing up). Here, clams are steamed with wine, garlic, shallots, and herbs. If all the clams do not open at once, cook the unopened ones a minute or two longer; if they still don't open, discard them.

CAESAR SALAD

SERVES: 4
WORKING TIME: 15 MINUTES
TOTAL TIME: 15 MINUTES

The Italian chef Caesar Cardini devised this world-famous dish at his restaurant in Tijuana, Mexico, in the 1920s. In place of the traditional raw egg, we've used a little reduced-fat mayonnaise to add richness to the dressing. And to cut even more fat, the croutons are toasted instead of fried.

2 ounces Italian bread, cut into ½-inch cubes

3 tablespoons reduced-fat mayonnaise

2 tablespoons fresh lemon juice

2 tablespoons reduced-sodium chicken broth, defatted

1 teaspoon anchovy paste

½ teaspoon freshly ground black pepper

8 cups torn romaine lettuce

15½-ounce can red kidney beans, rinsed and drained

¼ cup grated Parmesan cheese

1. In a toaster oven or under the broiler, toast the bread cubes for about 1 minute, or until golden.

2. In a large bowl, combine the mayonnaise, lemon juice, broth, anchovy paste, and ¼ teaspoon of the pepper, whisking until smooth and blended.

3. Add the lettuce, beans, bread cubes, and Parmesan, tossing to coat thoroughly with the dressing. Sprinkle with the remaining ¼ teaspoon pepper and serve.

Helpful hint: You can make the dressing up to 12 hours in advance and store it in a covered jar. Shake or whisk the dressing again before pouring it over the salad.

FAT: 5G/23%
CALORIES: 193
SATURATED FAT: 1.5G
CARBOHYDRATE: 25G
PROTEIN: 11G
CHOLESTEROL: 5MG
SODIUM: 487MG

PROSCIUTTO AND MELON

The city of Parma and its environs have given the world two great delicacies: Parmesan cheese and prosciutto di Parma, a painstakingly produced air-dried ham. Even with just half an ounce of prosciutto on each of these delicious honeydew melon wedges, the unique combination of flavors is sure to please. Garnish with two teaspoons of grated lime zest, if you like.

¼ cup sugar
¼ cup fresh lime juice
½ of a honeydew melon, chilled
2 ounces very thinly sliced prosciutto, cut into thin strips
¼ teaspoon freshly ground black pepper

1. In a small saucepan, combine the sugar, lime juice, and ¼ cup of water. Bring to a boil over medium heat, reduce to a simmer, and cook until syrupy, about 12 minutes. Set aside to cool slightly.

2. Cut the melon into 4 even wedges. With a sharp paring knife, score the melon wedges crosswise at ½-inch intervals, cutting to, but not through, the rind. Place the melon on a serving platter and spoon the lime syrup over each wedge. Sprinkle the prosciutto and pepper over the melon and serve.

Helpful hint: For a change, serve the prosciutto with cantaloupe quarters instead of honeydew wedges.

FAT: 2G/13%
CALORIES: 143
SATURATED FAT: .5G
CARBOHYDRATE: 29G
PROTEIN: 5G
CHOLESTEROL: 12MG
SODIUM: 279MG

Roasted Pepper and Tomato Antipasto

SERVES: 4
WORKING TIME: 25 MINUTES
TOTAL TIME: 25 MINUTES

In a traditional Italian meal, the appetite-honing delights that precede the pasta course—known as antipasti—must please the eye as well as the palate. These golden roasted peppers layered over lush ripe tomatoes certainly fill the bill. Accompany the peppers with sesame-seeded semolina bread. This first course could also be served as a side dish with meat or poultry.

2 red or yellow bell peppers, quartered lengthwise and seeded

2 large tomatoes, sliced

½ cup slivered red onion

2 tablespoons balsamic vinegar

½ teaspoon salt

¼ teaspoon freshly ground black pepper

3 tablespoons shredded part-skim mozzarella or smoked mozzarella cheese

1. Preheat the broiler. Place the bell peppers, cut-sides down, on the broiler rack. Broil the peppers 4 inches from the heat for 12 minutes, or until the skins are blackened. When the peppers are cool enough to handle, remove the skins.

2. On a serving platter, arrange the peppers, tomatoes, and onion. Sprinkle with the vinegar, salt, and black pepper, top with the mozzarella, and serve.

Helpful hint: Double or triple this recipe for a party, using a colorful mix of red and yellow peppers.

FAT: 1G/18%
CALORIES: 49
SATURATED FAT: .6G
CARBOHYDRATE: 8G
PROTEIN: 3G
CHOLESTEROL: 3MG
SODIUM: 308MG

SHRIMP WITH FENNEL AND TOMATOES

SERVES: 4
WORKING TIME: 35 MINUTES
TOTAL TIME: 40 MINUTES

1 tablespoon olive oil

1 small fennel bulb, trimmed and thinly sliced, fronds reserved and chopped

2 cloves garlic, thinly sliced

½ cup orange juice

2 cups chopped tomatoes

½ teaspoon salt

1 pound large shrimp, shelled and deveined

1. In a large nonstick skillet, heat the oil until hot but not smoking over medium heat. Add the sliced fennel and garlic and cook, stirring frequently, until the fennel is tender, about 7 minutes. Add the orange juice, bring to a boil, and cook until the orange juice is almost absorbed, about 4 minutes.

2. Stir the tomatoes and salt into the pan and cook, stirring frequently, until the sauce is richly flavored and slightly reduced, about 5 minutes. Add the shrimp and cook until the shrimp are just opaque, about 3 minutes. Spoon onto 4 plates, sprinkle with the fennel fronds, and serve.

Helpful hint: To prepare the fennel, cut off the stalks, reserving the fronds, and trim off the base of the bulb. Then cut the bulb crosswise into thin strips.

When fennel appears on the market in the fall, choose a bulb that has its stalks and feathery fronds still attached and treat yourself to this Sicilian-inspired dish. The gentle anise-like flavor of fennel is uniquely compatible with fish and shellfish. Offer bread, rolls, or bread sticks to sop up the delicious sauce.

FAT: 5G/26%
CALORIES: 171
SATURATED FAT: .8G
CARBOHYDRATE: 10G
PROTEIN: 20G
CHOLESTEROL: 140MG
SODIUM: 469MG

TUNA, BEET, AND POTATO ANTIPASTO

SERVES: 6
WORKING TIME: 25 MINUTES
TOTAL TIME: 40 MINUTES

Mashed potatoes and Dijon mustard—rather than fatty mayonnaise—give the dressing for this antipasto its thick texture.

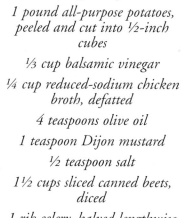

2 cloves garlic, peeled

1 pound all-purpose potatoes, peeled and cut into ½-inch cubes

⅓ cup balsamic vinegar

¼ cup reduced-sodium chicken broth, defatted

4 teaspoons olive oil

1 teaspoon Dijon mustard

½ teaspoon salt

1½ cups sliced canned beets, diced

1 rib celery, halved lengthwise and thinly sliced

6½-ounce can water-packed tuna, drained

1 tablespoon capers, rinsed and drained

2 cups watercress or arugula leaves

2 cups torn Boston lettuce

1. In a large pot of boiling water, cook the garlic for 2 minutes to blanch. With a slotted spoon, transfer the garlic to a large bowl and set aside. Add the potatoes to the boiling water and cook until tender, about 15 minutes. Drain.

2. Transfer ½ cup of the potatoes to the bowl and mash with the garlic. Stir in the vinegar, broth, oil, mustard, and salt. Add the remaining potatoes, the beets, celery, tuna, and capers, tossing to combine. Line 6 plates with the watercress and Boston lettuce. Top with the tuna and potato mixture and serve warm, at room temperature, or chilled.

Helpful hint: For a robust salad, use light tuna. If you prefer a more delicate flavor, choose solid white tuna.

FAT: 3G/21%
CALORIES: 131
SATURATED FAT: .5G
CARBOHYDRATE: 15G
PROTEIN: 10G
CHOLESTEROL: 12MG
SODIUM: 480MG

PASTA E FAGIOLI

SERVES: 6
WORKING TIME: 45 MINUTES
TOTAL TIME: 45 MINUTES

1 teaspoon olive oil

1 onion, chopped

2 ribs celery, diced

1 carrot, quartered lengthwise
and sliced

2 cloves garlic, minced

3 cups reduced-sodium chicken
broth, defatted

½ cup dry white wine

2 teaspoons dried rosemary

¾ teaspoon dried thyme

1 cup diced red potatoes

¼ pound green beans, cut into
1-inch pieces

½ cup ditalini pasta

19-ounce can chick-peas, rinsed
and drained

2 tablespoons chopped
prosciutto or Canadian bacon

¼ teaspoon freshly ground
black pepper

1. In a medium nonstick saucepan, heat the oil until hot but not smoking over medium heat. Add the onion, celery, and carrot and cook, stirring occasionally, until the vegetables are softened, about 5 minutes. Add the garlic and cook until fragrant, about 1 minute.

2. Add the broth, 2 cups of water, the wine, rosemary, thyme, and potatoes. Bring to a simmer and cook 5 minutes. Add the green beans and pasta and simmer, covered, until the beans are crisp-tender, about 8 minutes. Add the chick-peas, prosciutto, and pepper and cook until warmed through, about 3 minutes. Divide the mixture among 6 bowls and serve.

Helpful hints: Like all good country recipes, this one is quite amenable to the substitution of similar ingredients. Cannellini (white kidney beans) can replace the chick-peas, and tiny elbow macaroni (or even broken spaghetti) can stand in for the thimble-shaped ditalini.

FAT: 3G/15%
CALORIES: 181
SATURATED FAT: .4G
CARBOHYDRATE: 27G
PROTEIN: 9G
CHOLESTEROL: 4MG
SODIUM: 531MG

For a warming yet light supper, serve this classic bean soup with wedges of Italian focaccia or with bread sticks.

ONION AND TOMATO PIZZA

SERVES: 6
WORKING TIME: 45 MINUTES
TOTAL TIME: 55 MINUTES

Pizza

can be quite healthy

if the crust isn't

buried under a thick

layer of cheese, sausage,

and pepperoni. We've

crowned this one

with juicy fresh

tomatoes, savory-sweet

braised onions, and

a sprinkling of

Parmesan. The crust,

made with baking

powder instead of

yeast, is quickly

prepared, yet still light

and crusty.

2 tablespoons plus 2 teaspoons olive oil

4 cups slivered onions

1 teaspoon sugar

½ cup reduced-sodium chicken broth, defatted

¼ cup chopped fresh basil

¼ teaspoon freshly ground black pepper

2 cups flour

1 tablespoon baking powder

¾ teaspoon salt

¾ cup skim milk

1 tablespoon fresh lemon juice

2 large tomatoes, thinly sliced

3 tablespoons grated Parmesan cheese

1. In a large nonstick skillet, heat 2 teaspoons of the oil until hot but not smoking over medium heat. Add the onions and sugar and cook, stirring frequently, until the onions begin to brown, about 12 minutes. Add the broth and cook until the onions are browned and all the liquid has been absorbed, about 15 minutes. Stir in the basil and pepper.

2. Meanwhile, preheat the oven to 425°. Lightly spray a 12-inch pizza pan with nonstick cooking spray. In a large bowl, combine the flour, baking powder, and salt. Make a well in the center of the flour mixture and add the milk, the remaining 2 tablespoons oil, and the lemon juice to the center. Stir the dry ingredients into the wet until just combined. Do not overmix. Form the dough into a loose ball and gently roll it out on a lightly floured surface to an 11-inch round. Transfer the dough to the prepared pan, gently pressing with your fingertips so the dough fully fits the pan.

3. Bake the pizza base for 5 minutes. Remove it from the oven and spread the onion mixture over it. Top with the sliced tomatoes and sprinkle with the Parmesan. Return to the oven and bake for 6 to 7 minutes, or until the cheese has melted and the crust is golden brown.

FAT: 8G/25%
CALORIES: 287
SATURATED FAT: 1.4G
CARBOHYDRATE: 47G
PROTEIN: 8G
CHOLESTEROL: 3MG
SODIUM: 643MG

CAPONATA

SERVES: 4
WORKING TIME: 25 MINUTES
TOTAL TIME: 40 MINUTES

This Sicilian vegetable dish resembles ratatouille, but it's considerably more tangy than its Provençal counterpart. Surround the caponata with a generous assortment of raw vegetable dippers—celery, carrots, and bell peppers—along with some seeded bread sticks. Or serve low-fat crackers or quartered slices of peasant bread alongside.

2 teaspoons olive oil

1 cup diced onion

1 garlic clove, minced

3 cups peeled, diced eggplant (about 9 ounces)

2 cups chopped tomatoes

1 cup diced celery

¾ cup reduced-sodium chicken broth, defatted

2 tablespoons no-salt-added tomato paste

½ teaspoon salt

¼ teaspoon freshly ground black pepper

1 tablespoon capers, rinsed, drained, and chopped

2 teaspoons red wine vinegar

1. In a large nonstick skillet, heat the oil until hot but not smoking over medium-high heat. Add the onion and garlic and cook until the onion is softened, about 5 minutes.

2. Add the eggplant, 1 cup of the tomatoes, the celery, broth, ¾ cup of water, the tomato paste, salt, and pepper. Bring to a boil, reduce to a simmer, and cook until the sauce is thickened and the vegetables are softened, about 15 minutes.

3. Stir in the remaining 1 cup tomatoes, the capers, and vinegar. Spoon the caponata into a serving bowl and serve warm, at room temperature, or chilled.

Helpful hint: To peel the eggplant, use a swivel-bladed vegetable peeler and don't peel until just before cooking. The eggplant flesh will quickly darken once it's peeled.

FAT: 3G/29%
CALORIES: 87
SATURATED FAT: .4G
CARBOHYDRATE: 15G
PROTEIN: 3G
CHOLESTEROL: 0MG
SODIUM: 493MG

Lemon-Garlic Mushrooms

Serves: 4
Working time: 30 minutes
Total time: 30 minutes

2 slices (1 ounce each) white sandwich bread, torn into large pieces

2 pounds mushrooms, quartered

1 cup reduced-sodium chicken broth, defatted

2 cloves garlic, peeled

¼ cup fresh lemon juice

2 teaspoons olive oil

½ teaspoon salt

¼ teaspoon freshly ground black pepper

2 tablespoons chopped fresh parsley

1 teaspoon grated lemon zest

1. Preheat the broiler. In a food processor or blender, process the bread just until coarse crumbs form. Spread the bread crumbs on a baking sheet and broil for 30 seconds to lightly toast. Set aside.

2. In a medium saucepan, combine the mushrooms and broth. Bring to a boil over medium-high heat, reduce to a simmer, and cook until the mushrooms are tender, about 10 minutes. Reserving ¼ cup of the broth, drain the mushrooms and set aside to cool slightly.

3. Meanwhile, in a small pot of boiling water, cook the garlic for 2 minutes to blanch. Transfer the garlic to a cutting board and mince. In a large bowl, combine the reserved broth, the lemon juice, oil, half of the garlic, the salt, and pepper, whisking well to blend. Add the cooled mushrooms, stirring to coat thoroughly.

4. In a small bowl, combine the bread crumbs, parsley, lemon zest, and the remaining garlic. Spoon the mushrooms into a serving dish and sprinkle with the topping. Serve at room temperature.

Helpful hint: Slightly stale or very lightly toasted bread makes the best crumbs. If you don't have a food processor, you can use your fingers to tear the bread into fluffy crumbs.

Fat: 4g/29%
Calories: 126
Saturated Fat: .5g
Carbohydrate: 20g
Protein: 7g
Cholesterol: 0mg
Sodium: 521mg

Stuffed mushroom caps are great for parties, but they can require a fair amount of fuss and fiddling. This mushroom salad captures the flavors of stuffed mushrooms— right down to the garlicky bread crumbs—without the time-consuming preparation. Try this dish as a component of a buffet centered around smoked turkey or ham.

Perhaps you've sampled focaccia in a restaurant: This thick, chewy Italian flatbread—much like a pizza crust—has gained popularity in recent years. Our rosemary-scented version, studded with bits of sun-dried tomato, is delicious as a snack or as a soup or salad accompaniment. You can use leftovers to make spectacular sandwiches.

ROSEMARY FOCACCIA

SERVES: 8
WORKING TIME: 20 MINUTES
TOTAL TIME: 1 HOUR 35 MINUTES

¼ cup sun-dried (not oil-packed)
tomato halves

4½ cups flour

⅔ cup grated Parmesan cheese

1 package rapid-rise yeast

2 teaspoons dried rosemary

1 teaspoon sugar

½ teaspoon salt

½ teaspoon freshly ground black
pepper

1⅓ cups very warm water
(120° to 130°)

3 tablespoons plus 2 teaspoons
olive oil

1. In a small pot of boiling water, cook the sun-dried tomatoes until softened, about 4 minutes. Drain well and finely chop.

2. In a large bowl, combine 4 cups of the flour, ⅓ cup of the Parmesan, the sun-dried tomatoes, yeast, 1 teaspoon of the rosemary, the sugar, salt, and pepper. Make a well in the center of the flour mixture and add the warm water and 3 tablespoons of the oil to the center. Stir the dry ingredients into the wet until just combined. Do not overmix. Transfer the dough to a lightly floured board and knead for about 8 minutes, adding as much of the remaining ½ cup flour as needed to make the dough smooth and elastic.

3. Spray a 15 x 11-inch jelly-roll pan with nonstick cooking spray. Roll the dough out to a 15 x 11-inch rectangle and carefully fit the dough into the pan. Cover the dough with a kitchen towel and set aside in a warm place to rise until light and puffy, about 1 hour.

4. Preheat the oven to 425°. With your fingers, make indentations on the surface of the dough in a random pattern (see tip). Brush the top of the focaccia with the remaining 2 teaspoons oil and sprinkle with the remaining 1 teaspoon rosemary and remaining ⅓ cup Parmesan. Bake for 12 to 13 minutes, or until the focaccia is golden brown and sounds hollow when tapped. Cool on a wire rack. Cut the focaccia into 8 squares, then halve each square on the diagonal, for a total of 16 wedges.

FAT: 9G/23%
CALORIES: 354
SATURATED FAT: 2.2G
CARBOHYDRATE: 56G
PROTEIN: 11G
CHOLESTEROL: 5MG
SODIUM: 266MG

TIP

In a traditional focaccia, a random pattern of indentations is made in the dough before baking. This allows the flavorful olive oil and seasonings (in this case rosemary and Parmesan) to permeate the bread. To make the indentations, gently press down on the surface of the dough with your fingers without going all the way through.

BROILED SHRIMP WITH LEMON AND BASIL

SERVES: 4
WORKING TIME: 25 MINUTES
TOTAL TIME: 30 MINUTES PLUS MARINATING TIME

Italian cooks season many foods with the simple and elegant combination of lemon, garlic, and olive oil. Here, this traditional blend of flavors—enhanced by the addition of fresh basil and a hint of vermouth—serves as a marinade for broiled shrimp. In the summer, skewer the shrimp and grill them outdoors.

¼ cup chopped fresh basil

2 cloves garlic, minced

2 tablespoons dry vermouth or vodka

1 tablespoon olive oil

1 teaspoon grated lemon zest

2 tablespoons fresh lemon juice

½ teaspoon dried oregano

¼ teaspoon salt

¼ teaspoon freshly ground black pepper

1 pound large shrimp, shelled and deveined

4 ounces Italian bread, cut into 8 slices

1. In a large bowl, combine the basil, garlic, vermouth, oil, lemon zest, lemon juice, oregano, salt, and pepper. Add the shrimp, tossing to coat. Set aside to marinate for at least 30 minutes at room temperature or for up to 4 hours in the refrigerator.

2. Preheat the broiler or grill. Under the broiler or on the grill, toast the bread on one side. Set aside. Broil or grill the shrimp 6 inches from the heat, turning once, for 3 minutes, or until just opaque.

3. Place 2 slices of toast on each of 4 plates. Top with the shrimp and serve.

Helpful hint: For extra flavor, rub the bread slices with a halved clove of peeled garlic before toasting them.

FAT: 6G/24%
CALORIES: 222
SATURATED FAT: 1G
CARBOHYDRATE: 17G
PROTEIN: 22G
CHOLESTEROL: 140MG
SODIUM: 438MG

POTATO-ONION ANTIPASTO

SERVES: 4
WORKING TIME: 30 MINUTES
TOTAL TIME: 30 MINUTES

In some ways, this first course resembles a classic American potato salad, with hard-cooked eggs and celery for textural contrast. But this Italian version is dressed with a mustardy red-wine vinaigrette and served on a bed of slivered onions and tomatoes. It's a great starter for your next al fresco meal—or even for a plain old American picnic.

1 pound small red potatoes, cut into ½-inch dice
1 egg
2 tablespoons red wine vinegar
1 tablespoon extra-virgin olive oil
2 teaspoons Dijon mustard
½ teaspoon salt
¼ teaspoon freshly ground black pepper
2 ribs celery, diced
2 tablespoons chopped fresh parsley
2 tomatoes, thinly sliced
½ cup slivered red onion

1. In a large pot of boiling water, cook the potatoes until firm-tender, about 9 minutes. Drain.

2. Meanwhile, place the egg in a saucepan, add cold water to cover by 1 inch, and bring to a boil over medium-high heat. As soon as the water comes to a boil, cover the pan, remove from the heat, and let stand for 17 minutes. Peel the egg under cold running water and coarsely chop.

3. In a large bowl, combine the vinegar, oil, mustard, salt, and pepper, whisking well. Stir in the potatoes, celery, and parsley.

4. Arrange the tomatoes and onion on a serving platter. Spoon the potato mixture on top, sprinkle with the egg, and serve.

Helpful hint: If you find the flavor of raw onions too sharp, drop the slivered onions into a bowl of cold water and place them in the freezer for 15 minutes. They'll emerge noticeably milder. Drain the onions and pat them dry before using.

FAT: 5G/27%
CALORIES: 169
SATURATED FAT: .9G
CARBOHYDRATE: 26G
PROTEIN: 5G
CHOLESTEROL: 53MG
SODIUM: 384MG

Homemade Italian Sausage Patties

SERVES: 4
WORKING TIME: 25 MINUTES
TOTAL TIME: 25 MINUTES

These miniature chicken-and-pork patties—flavored with Italian seasonings like fennel and sage—are delicious low-fat treats.

2 slices (1 ounce each) white sandwich bread

6 ounces skinless, boneless chicken breast, cut into small pieces

2 ounces lean ground pork

1 teaspoon fennel seeds, crushed

¼ teaspoon dried sage

1 teaspoon grated orange zest

½ teaspoon salt

¼ teaspoon freshly ground black pepper

1 egg white, beaten

3 ounces Italian bread, cut into 8 slices

½ cup jarred roasted red peppers, drained and cut into thin strips

1. Preheat the broiler. In a food processor or blender, process the sandwich bread just until coarse crumbs form. Transfer the crumbs to a large bowl and set aside. Add the chicken to the processor and process until coarsely ground, about 30 seconds.

2. Add the chicken to the bread crumbs along with the pork, fennel seeds, sage, orange zest, salt, black pepper, and egg white, mixing thoroughly. Shape the mixture into 8 round, flat patties. Broil the sausage patties 6 inches from the heat, turning once, for 6 minutes, or until cooked through.

3. Broil the Italian bread slices for 30 seconds per side, until lightly toasted. Dividing evenly, spoon the roasted red peppers over the toast. Top each piece with a sausage patty and serve.

Helpful hint: If you'd like to grind your own pork, you can use either 2 ounces of pork tenderloin, or 2 ounces of meat trimmed from a lean pork chop. Cut the pork into small pieces and add to the food processor along with the chicken in step 1.

FAT: 3G/15%
CALORIES: 175
SATURATED FAT: .7G
CARBOHYDRATE: 19G
PROTEIN: 17G
CHOLESTEROL: 33MG
SODIUM: 559MG

PASTA

2

PENNE WITH SPINACH AND CHICK-PEAS

SERVES: 4
WORKING TIME: 35 MINUTES
TOTAL TIME: 40 MINUTES

You might not see a lot of sauce in this tricolored pasta dish, but you'll be wowed by the flavor. The pungency of garlic is played against the freshness of orange and the subtlety of sage, while nutmeg brings out the best in the spinach. If you've never cooked with fresh nutmeg, buy yourself a whole nutmeg and a nutmeg grater and prepare for an eye-opener.

10 ounces penne pasta
1 tablespoon olive oil
1 large onion, diced
3 cloves garlic, minced
1 large red bell pepper, diced
16-ounce can chick-peas, rinsed and drained
8 cups torn fresh spinach leaves (about 1 pound)
1 cup reduced-sodium chicken broth, defatted
½ teaspoon grated orange zest
¾ teaspoon salt
¼ teaspoon dried sage
¼ teaspoon nutmeg
1 teaspoon cornstarch mixed with 1 tablespoon water

1. In a large pot of boiling water, cook the penne until just tender. Drain well.

2. Meanwhile, in a large nonstick skillet, heat the oil until hot but not smoking over medium heat. Add the onion and garlic and cook, stirring occasionally, until the onion is softened, about 7 minutes. Add the bell pepper and cook, stirring occasionally, until the bell pepper is softened, about 5 minutes.

3. Stir the chick-peas, spinach, broth, orange zest, salt, sage, and nutmeg into the skillet and simmer gently until the spinach is wilted, about 5 minutes. Bring to a boil, stir in the cornstarch mixture, and cook, stirring constantly, until slightly thickened, about 1 minute. Combine the penne and the chick-pea mixture in a large bowl, tossing to coat. Divide among 4 bowls and serve.

Helpful hint: Chick-peas, which look like small, cream-colored hazelnuts, may also be labeled "garbanzos" (their Spanish name) or "ceci" (their Italian name).

FAT: 7G/15%
CALORIES: 435
SATURATED FAT: .8G
CARBOHYDRATE: 76G
PROTEIN: 18G
CHOLESTEROL: 0MG
SODIUM: 795MG

FETTUCCINE WITH SHRIMP AND LEMON CREAM SAUCE

SERVES: 4
WORKING TIME: 30 MINUTES
TOTAL TIME: 35 MINUTES

There could hardly be a quicker, easier dinner-party dish—or a more welcome weekday treat for the family—than this luscious pairing of seafood and pasta. The rich-but-slim sauce gets its velvety consistency from evaporated low-fat milk and cornstarch. Any thick, long-stranded fresh pasta (such as linguine or long fusilli) will complement the sauce nicely.

2 teaspoons olive oil

1 pound medium shrimp, shelled and deveined

3 cloves garlic, minced

12 ounces fresh spinach fettuccine

2 tablespoons fresh lemon juice

¾ cup reduced-sodium chicken broth, defatted

1 cup evaporated low-fat milk

¾ teaspoon grated lemon zest

½ teaspoon salt

1½ teaspoons cornstarch mixed with 1 tablespoon water

¼ cup chopped fresh parsley

1. Start heating a large pot of water to boiling for the pasta. In a large nonstick skillet, heat the oil until hot but not smoking over medium heat. Add the shrimp and garlic and cook, stirring occasionally, until the shrimp are opaque on the outside but still translucent in the center, about 2 minutes. With a slotted spoon, transfer the shrimp to a plate. Set aside.

2. Cook the fettuccine in the boiling water until just tender. Drain well.

3. Meanwhile, add the lemon juice to the skillet, stirring to incorporate the garlic. Add the broth and cook for 1 minute to blend the flavors. Stir in the milk, lemon zest, and salt and bring to a boil. Stir in the cornstarch mixture and cook, stirring constantly, until slightly thickened, about 1 minute. Return the shrimp to the skillet and cook until opaque throughout. Add the parsley and transfer to a large bowl. Add the fettuccine, toss well, and serve.

Helpful hint: Fresh pasta cooks in much less time than dried; check it frequently to avoid overcooking.

FAT: 9G/16%
CALORIES: 510
SATURATED FAT: 1.5G
CARBOHYDRATE: 70G
PROTEIN: 36G
CHOLESTEROL: 231MG
SODIUM: 659MG

PASTA SHELLS WITH SAUSAGE AND MUSHROOMS

SERVES: 4
WORKING TIME: 35 MINUTES
TOTAL TIME: 40 MINUTES

½ ounce dried mushrooms,
preferably porcini

1½ cups boiling water

10 ounces medium pasta shells

2 teaspoons olive oil

½ pound Italian-style turkey
sausage, casings removed

4 shallots or scallions, finely
chopped

2 cloves garlic, minced

1 large yellow or red bell pepper,
cut into 1-inch squares

½ pound fresh mushrooms,
thickly sliced

1 large tomato, coarsely chopped

½ teaspoon salt

⅓ cup grated Parmesan cheese

1. In a small bowl, combine the dried mushrooms and boiling water and let stand until softened, about 10 minutes. Remove the dried mushrooms from their soaking liquid, reserving the liquid. Rinse and coarsely chop the mushrooms. Strain the liquid through a paper towel-lined sieve and set aside.

2. In a large pot of boiling water, cook the pasta shells until just tender. Drain well.

3. Meanwhile, in a large nonstick skillet, heat 1 teaspoon of the oil until hot but not smoking over medium heat. Crumble the sausage into the pan and cook until lightly golden, about 3 minutes. With a slotted spoon, transfer the sausage to a plate. Add the shallots and garlic to the pan and cook, stirring frequently, until the shallots are softened, about 2 minutes.

4. Add the remaining 1 teaspoon oil to the pan along with the bell pepper, fresh mushrooms, and dried mushrooms and cook, stirring occasionally, until the pepper and fresh mushrooms are tender, about 5 minutes. Stir in the tomato, reserved mushroom soaking liquid, and salt. Return the sausage to the pan and simmer until the sausage is cooked through, about 4 minutes. Toss with the pasta and Parmesan, divide the mixture among 4 plates, and serve.

FAT: 12G/24%
CALORIES: 455
SATURATED FAT: 3.4G
CARBOHYDRATE: 65G
PROTEIN: 24G
CHOLESTEROL: 36MG
SODIUM: 782MG

The savory sauce for this delicious pasta dish pays double homage to the Italian passion for mushrooms—dried mushrooms (use Italian porcini if you can) are paired with fresh white button mushrooms to simulate the taste and texture of fresh porcini. The turkey sausage offers a light alternative to traditional pork sausage.

*W*hat are fruit and nuts doing in a pasta sauce? The pear's delicate sweetness is a lovely complement to the Fontina, and the pistachios underscore the nutlike aspect of the cheese's flavor. Radiatore pasta is the perfect choice to catch and hold the creamy sauce; though cavatappi (hollow corkscrew pasta) or small shells would also work well.

RADIATORE WITH CREAMY FONTINA SAUCE

SERVES: 4
WORKING TIME: 20 MINUTES
TOTAL TIME: 30 MINUTES

10 ounces radiatore pasta

3 tablespoons flour

1 teaspoon salt

¼ teaspoon freshly ground black
pepper

⅛ teaspoon cayenne pepper

2 cups low-fat (1%) milk

1 medium firm ripe pear, peeled,
cored, and diced

¾ cup (3 ounces) shredded
Fontina cheese (see tip)

1 cup frozen peas, thawed

1 tablespoon coarsely chopped
shelled pistachio nuts

¼ cup chopped fresh parsley

1. In a large pot of boiling water, cook the radiatore until just tender. Drain well.

2. Meanwhile, in a large saucepan, combine the flour, salt, black pepper, and cayenne, whisking well. Gradually whisk the milk into the flour mixture. Bring to a boil over medium heat, add the pear, and cook, stirring constantly, until the sauce is slightly thickened and the pear is softened, about 5 minutes. Stir in the Fontina and cook until just melted, about 2 minutes.

3. Add the peas, pistachios, and parsley and cook just until the peas are warmed through, about 2 minutes. Combine the penne with the sauce, divide among 4 bowls, and serve.

Helpful hints: You can substitute walnuts or pine nuts for the pistachios and a mild Monterey jack for the Fontina, if you like.

FAT: 10G/19%
CALORIES: 484
SATURATED FAT: 5.2G
CARBOHYDRATE: 76G
PROTEIN: 22G
CHOLESTEROL: 30MG
SODIUM: 828MG

FUSILLI WITH TUNA AND PINE NUTS

SERVES: 4
WORKING TIME: 30 MINUTES
TOTAL TIME: 35 MINUTES

The effect this dish will have on your taste buds can be best described as "fireworks." Not because it's super-hot (although the red pepper flakes do pack a punch), but because of the wide variety of flavors—tuna, garlic, pine nuts, capers, basil, oregano, parsley, and lemon. Serve it with a simple salad of tender leaf lettuces (to give your palate a rest from all the excitement).

12 ounces fusilli pasta
1 teaspoon olive oil
1 red bell pepper, diced
4 scallions, finely chopped
3 cloves garlic, minced
¾ teaspoon dried basil
½ teaspoon dried oregano
Two 8-ounce bottles clam juice
¼ cup dry white wine
½ teaspoon red pepper flakes
1 teaspoon anchovy paste
2 teaspoons cornstarch mixed with 1 tablespoon water
2 tablespoons pine nuts, toasted
2 tablespoons capers, rinsed and drained
6-ounce can water-packed tuna, drained and flaked
¼ cup chopped fresh parsley
2 tablespoons fresh lemon juice

1. In a large pot of boiling water, cook the fusilli until just tender. Drain well.

2. Meanwhile, in a large nonstick saucepan, heat the oil until hot but not smoking over medium heat. Add the bell pepper and cook until crisp-tender, about 4 minutes. Add the scallions, garlic, basil, and oregano and cook until warmed through, about 3 minutes.

3. Add the clam juice, wine, red pepper flakes, and anchovy paste. Bring to a simmer and cook for 4 minutes to reduce slightly. Stir in the cornstarch mixture and cook, stirring, until slightly thickened, about 2 minutes.

4. Remove the pan from the heat and stir in the pine nuts, capers, tuna, parsley, and lemon juice. Add the pasta, toss well, and let stand for 5 minutes to absorb the liquid. Divide the mixture among 4 bowls and serve.

Helpful hint: To toast the pine nuts, spread them out on a small baking pan and cook them in a 350° oven for 8 to 10 minutes; shake the pan occasionally to keep the nuts from scorching, and turn them out of the pan as soon as they're done.

FAT: 5G/10%
CALORIES: 437
SATURATED FAT: .8G
CARBOHYDRATE: 70G
PROTEIN: 25G
CHOLESTEROL: 17MG
SODIUM: 570MG

LINGUINE WITH BEEF AND CARAMELIZED ONIONS

SERVES: 4
WORKING TIME: 30 MINUTES
TOTAL TIME: 40 MINUTES

Diced sirloin makes a most luxurious meat sauce in this traditional dish, and sherry adds a subtle, graceful note.

1 tablespoon olive oil

1½ tablespoons finely chopped pancetta or Canadian bacon

3 large onions, coarsely chopped

3 cloves garlic, minced

1 large carrot, finely chopped

10 ounces linguine

¼ cup dry sherry

1 cup reduced-sodium chicken broth, defatted

¾ teaspoon salt

½ teaspoon dried oregano

¼ teaspoon freshly ground black pepper

6 ounces well-trimmed sirloin, cut into ¼-inch dice

2 tablespoons flour

2 tablespoons grated Parmesan cheese

1. Bring a large pot of boiling water to a boil for the pasta. In a large nonstick skillet, heat the oil until hot but not smoking over medium heat. Add the pancetta and cook until lightly crisped, about 1 minute. Add the onions and garlic and cook, stirring frequently, until the onions are golden brown, about 10 minutes. Add the carrot and cook, stirring frequently, until the carrot is tender, about 5 minutes.

2. Meanwhile, in a large pot of boiling water, cook the linguine until tender. Drain well.

3. Add the sherry to the skillet, increase the heat to high, and cook until the sherry has evaporated, about 2 minutes. Stir in the broth, salt, oregano, and pepper and reduce the heat to medium. Add the meat, stirring to coat. Sprinkle the flour on top, stirring until the meat is well coated. Cook, stirring frequently, until the sauce is slightly thickened and the meat is cooked through, about 3 minutes. Transfer to a large bowl, add the linguine, and toss well to combine. Add the Parmesan, toss again, divide the mixture among 4 bowls, and serve.

Helpful hint: Sherry comes in varying degrees of sweetness: Choose a dry sherry for use in savory dishes such as this one—Manzanilla and fino are among the best.

FAT: 8G/15%
CALORIES: 482
SATURATED FAT: 1.9G
CARBOHYDRATE: 75G
PROTEIN: 23G
CHOLESTEROL: 30MG
SODIUM: 712MG

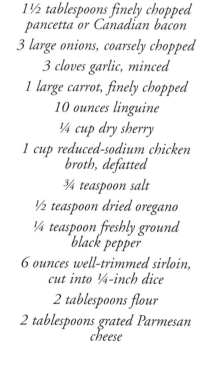

Farfalle with Codfish and Spicy Tomato Sauce

SERVES: 4
WORKING TIME: 30 MINUTES
TOTAL TIME: 40 MINUTES

2 tablespoons flour

1 pound cod fillets, cut into 8 chunks

1 tablespoon olive oil

10 ounces farfalle pasta

1 large yellow or red bell pepper, diced

2 cloves garlic, minced

½ cup Marsala wine

3 tomatoes, coarsely chopped

2 tablespoons no-salt-added tomato paste

¼ cup chopped fresh mint

¾ teaspoon salt

¼ to ½ teaspoon hot pepper sauce

1 teaspoon cornstarch mixed with 1 tablespoon water

1. Start heating a large pot of water to boiling for the pasta. Place the flour on a sheet of waxed paper and dredge the cod in the flour, shaking off the excess. In a large nonstick skillet, heat the oil until hot but not smoking over medium heat. Cook the cod until golden brown and lightly crisped, about 3 minutes per side. With a slotted spatula, transfer the cod to a plate.

2. Cook the farfalle in the boiling water until just tender. Drain well. Meanwhile, add the bell pepper and garlic to the skillet and cook, stirring frequently, until the pepper is tender, about 4 minutes. Stir in the Marsala and cook until slightly reduced, about 2 minutes. Add the tomatoes, tomato paste, mint, salt, and hot pepper sauce and bring to a boil. Reduce to a simmer and cook, uncovered, until the sauce is richly flavored, about 7 minutes.

3. Return the sauce to a boil, stir in the cornstarch mixture, and cook, stirring, until slightly thickened, about 1 minute. Transfer the sauce to a large bowl and add the pasta and cod, tossing gently to combine. Spoon into 4 pasta bowls and serve.

Helpful hint: Marsala is a fortified wine made from Sicilian grapes and sweetened with concentrated grape juice. The driest Marsala is labeled "virgine." Dry sherry may be substituted, if necessary.

FAT: 6G/11%
CALORIES: 485
SATURATED FAT: .8G
CARBOHYDRATE: 68G
PROTEIN: 31G
CHOLESTEROL: 49MG
SODIUM: 508MG

I*n this dish, juicy nuggets of codfish are paired with pasta "butterflies" in an aromatic Marsala sauce.*

Straw and Hay with Pesto Alla Genovese

SERVES: 4
WORKING TIME: 25 MINUTES
TOTAL TIME: 40 MINUTES

The gold (straw) and green (hay) fettuccines are bathed here in a creamy pesto. In Genoa (pesto's "hometown"), pasta is combined with potatoes and green beans, then tossed with the basil sauce. Here, asparagus makes a delicious substitute for the beans. Follow the main dish with a classic Italian dessert of fresh figs and grapes.

3 cloves garlic, peeled

2 cups firmly packed fresh basil leaves

1 tablespoon olive oil

1 tablespoon pine nuts

¼ cup grated Parmesan cheese

2 tablespoons reduced-fat cream cheese (Neufchâtel)

⅔ cup reduced-sodium chicken broth, defatted

1 teaspoon salt

¼ teaspoon freshly ground black pepper

5 ounces plain fettuccine

5 ounces spinach fettuccine

½ pound all-purpose potatoes, peeled and cut into 1-inch cubes

¾ pound asparagus, tough ends trimmed, cut on the diagonal into 2-inch pieces

1. In a large pot of boiling water, cook the garlic for 2 minutes to blanch. With a slotted spoon, transfer the garlic to a food processor along with the basil, oil, pine nuts, Parmesan, cream cheese, broth, ¾ teaspoon of the salt, and the black pepper. Process to a smooth purée and transfer the pesto to a large bowl.

2. In the same pot, cook the fettuccine and potatoes with the remaining ¼ teaspoon salt until just tender. Add the asparagus to the pot for the last 2 minutes of cooking. Drain well and transfer to the bowl with the pesto, tossing to combine. Divide the mixture among 4 bowls and serve.

Helpful hint: If you're using fresh fettuccine, add it to the pot along with the asparagus in step 2 rather than with the potatoes, to avoid overcooking the pasta.

FAT: 11G/22%
CALORIES: 453
SATURATED FAT: 3.2G
CARBOHYDRATE: 73G
PROTEIN: 20G
CHOLESTEROL: 75MG
SODIUM: 832MG

LINGUINE WITH FRESH CLAMS IN RED SAUCE

SERVES: 4
WORKING TIME: 35 MINUTES
TOTAL TIME: 35 MINUTES

10 ounces fresh linguine

1 teaspoon olive oil

3 shallots or scallions, coarsely chopped

2 cloves garlic, minced

¼ cup dry red wine

1 bay leaf

½ teaspoon dried oregano

½ teaspoon dried basil

24 cherrystone clams

28-ounce can no-salt-added tomatoes, drained and finely chopped

1 tablespoon no-salt-added tomato paste

2 tablespoons chopped fresh parsley

1. In a large pot of boiling water, cook the linguine until just tender. Drain well.

2. Meanwhile, in a large nonstick skillet, heat the oil until hot but not smoking over medium heat. Add the shallots and garlic and cook until the shallots are softened, about 2 minutes. Add the wine, bay leaf, oregano, and basil and bring to a boil. Add the clams, cover, and cook until the clams open up, about 4 minutes. With a slotted spoon, transfer the clams to a bowl.

3. Add the tomatoes to the skillet along with the tomato paste. Cook, stirring occasionally, for 4 minutes to thicken slightly. Remove the bay leaf. Add the cooked pasta, tossing to coat. Transfer the pasta to a serving bowl, surround with the clams in their shells, sprinkle with the parsley, and serve.

Helpful hints: If any of the clams remain unopened after 4 minutes of cooking, remove the others and cook the unopened clams for 1 to 2 minutes longer. If they still do not open, discard them. If you prefer, use two 7¼-ounce cans of minced clams in place of the fresh clams.

FAT: 4G/10%
CALORIES: 355
SATURATED FAT: .5G
CARBOHYDRATE: 53G
PROTEIN: 24G
CHOLESTEROL: 87MG
SODIUM: 108MG

You may never open another can of clam sauce once you discover how easy it is to prepare this lavish seafood dinner. You could serve this dish as individual portions, but there's something particularly extravagant about presenting a big bowl brimming with the steaming linguine and succulent clams.

Peasant dishes are typically based on grains and vegetables, with small amounts of meat or cheese as flavorings. These healthy proportions are reflected in this rustic Italian meal: The hearty pasta and lentils are accented with touches of pancetta and Parmesan. Serve a lettuce and tomato salad with balsamic-vinegar dressing alongside.

Shells with Herbed Lentil Sauce

Serves: 4
Working time: 20 minutes
Total time: 50 minutes

1 teaspoon olive oil

3 tablespoons finely chopped pancetta or Canadian bacon (1 ounce)

1 large onion, finely chopped

2 cloves garlic, minced

1 large red bell pepper, diced

1 large carrot, halved lengthwise and thinly sliced

¾ cup lentils, rinsed and picked over

1¼ cups reduced-sodium chicken broth, defatted

½ teaspoon dried oregano

¼ teaspoon dried rosemary

¾ teaspoon salt

¼ teaspoon freshly ground black pepper

10 ounces medium pasta shells

¼ cup grated Parmesan cheese

⅓ cup chopped fresh parsley

2 teaspoons unsalted butter

1. In a medium nonstick saucepan, heat the oil until hot but not smoking over medium heat. Add the pancetta and cook until lightly crisped, about 1 minute. Add the onion and garlic and cook, stirring frequently, until the onions are softened, about 7 minutes.

2. Add the bell pepper and carrot to the pan and cook, stirring frequently, until tender, about 5 minutes. Stir in the lentils, broth, ½ cup of water, the oregano, rosemary, salt, and black pepper and bring to a boil. Reduce to a simmer, cover, and cook until the lentils are tender and most of the liquid has been absorbed, about 20 minutes (see tip).

3. Meanwhile, in a large pot of boiling water, cook the shells until just tender. Drain well. Transfer to a large bowl, add the lentil mixture, Parmesan, parsley, and butter. Toss well, divide among 4 plates, and serve.

Helpful hint: Although packaged lentils are usually quite clean, it's a good idea to look them over before cooking them. Pick out and discard any discolored lentils or bits of dirt, rinse thoroughly under cold running water, and drain.

Fat: 7g/13%
Calories: 495
Saturated Fat: 2.7g
Carbohydrate: 84g
Protein: 25g
Cholesterol: 13mg
Sodium: 828mg

TIP

The lentils should be cooked in a bit more liquid than they will eventually absorb. When they are done, all of the lentils at the top of the pot will seem dry, but there will still be some liquid at the bottom of the pot. The extra liquid, which has a meaty richness from the lentils, combines with the Parmesan, parsley, and butter to create a delicious sauce.

Roasted Vegetable Lasagna

SERVES: 4
WORKING TIME: 30 MINUTES
TOTAL TIME: 1 HOUR

The smoky succulence of roasted bell peppers and two kinds of summer squash give this meatless lasagna great depth of flavor. In warm weather, you could grill the vegetables over an outdoor fire. Placing the cooked lasagna noodles in a bowl of cold water keeps them from sticking together and tearing—saving wear and tear on the cook's temper as well.

9 lasagna noodles (9 ounces)

⅔ cup reduced-sodium chicken broth, defatted

3 tablespoons red wine vinegar

3 tablespoons no-salt-added tomato paste

¾ teaspoon dried oregano

½ teaspoon salt

¼ teaspoon freshly ground black pepper

2 zucchini, cut lengthwise into ¼-inch-thick slices

2 yellow summer squash, cut lengthwise into ¼-inch-thick slices

2 red bell peppers, cut into 1-inch-wide strips

Two 8-ounce cans no-salt-added tomato sauce

1½ cups shredded part-skim mozzarella cheese (6 ounces)

1. In a large pot of boiling water, cook the noodles until just tender. Drain well and transfer to a large bowl of cold water.

2. Preheat the broiler. In a large bowl, combine ⅓ cup of the broth, the vinegar, 1 tablespoon of the tomato paste, ¼ teaspoon of the oregano, ¼ teaspoon of the salt, and the black pepper. Add the zucchini and squash, stirring to combine. Place the zucchini, squash, and bell peppers on the broiler rack and broil 6 inches from the heat, turning occasionally, for 9 minutes, or until the zucchini and squash are tender and the bell pepper skins are blackened. When cool enough to handle, peel the pepper strips.

3. Preheat the oven to 375°. Spray an 11 x 7-inch baking dish with nonstick cooking spray. In a large bowl, combine the tomato sauce and the remaining ⅓ cup broth, 2 tablespoons tomato paste, ½ teaspoon oregano, and ¼ teaspoon salt.

4. Spoon 2 tablespoons of the tomato sauce onto the bottom of the baking dish. Make 2 layers, using the following order of ingredients: 3 noodles (the noodles will come up the ends of the baking dish), half of the vegetables, 1 cup of the sauce, ½ cup of the cheese. Make a final layer: 3 noodles, the remaining sauce, and the remaining cheese. Bake the lasagna for 20 minutes, or until bubbling hot. Let stand for 5 minutes, divide among 4 bowls, and serve.

FAT: 9G/19%
CALORIES: 439
SATURATED FAT: 4.5G
CARBOHYDRATE: 69G
PROTEIN: 23G
CHOLESTEROL: 25MG
SODIUM: 622MG

Rigatoni with Sun-Dried Tomato Pesto

Serves: 4
Working time: 25 minutes
Total time: 45 minutes

Hours of simmering and stirring are not the only route to a thick, rich tomato sauce. Here, flavor-packed sun-dried tomatoes, bell peppers, onion, and garlic are sautéed and then puréed to produce a vibrant tomato "pesto." The sauce coats chunky rigatoni, broccoli florets, and slivered black olives.

½ cup sun-dried (not oil-packed) tomato halves
1 cup boiling water
1 tablespoon olive oil
1 onion, halved and thinly sliced
2 red bell peppers, thinly sliced
2 cloves garlic, thinly sliced
½ cup reduced-sodium chicken broth, defatted
1 tablespoon balsamic vinegar
½ teaspoon salt
12 ounces rigatoni pasta
2 cups small broccoli florets
⅓ cup slivered Calamata or other brine-cured black olives

1. In a small bowl, combine the sun-dried tomatoes and boiling water and let stand until the tomatoes have softened, about 20 minutes. Drain the tomatoes, reserving the soaking liquid.

2. Meanwhile, in a large nonstick skillet, heat the oil until hot but not smoking over medium heat. Add the onion and cook, stirring occasionally, until golden brown, about 8 minutes. Add the bell peppers and garlic, stirring to combine. Add the broth and cook, stirring occasionally, until the peppers are softened, about 7 minutes. Transfer the mixture to a food processor along with the sun-dried tomatoes, the reserved soaking liquid, the vinegar and salt, and process until smooth, about 1 minute. Transfer the sauce to a large bowl.

3. In a large pot of boiling water, cook the rigatoni until just tender. Add the broccoli to the pot for the last 2 minutes of cooking. Drain well. Add the pasta and the broccoli to the sauce, tossing to combine. Add the olives, toss again, divide among 4 bowls, and serve.

Helpful hint: If you can't find Calamata olives, you can substitute Gaeta olives from Italy, or any other brine-cured (rather than oil-cured) black olives.

Fat: 8g/16%
Calories: 459
Saturated Fat: 1g
Carbohydrate: 81g
Protein: 16g
Cholesterol: 0mg
Sodium: 587mg

SUMMER PASTA WITH UNCOOKED TOMATO SAUCE

SERVES: 4
WORKING TIME: 25 MINUTES
TOTAL TIME: 25 MINUTES

eaty, ripe tomatoes (plum or beefsteak) and fresh mint or basil are necessities for this midsummer specialty.

4 cloves garlic, peeled

12 ounces spaghetti

2 pounds tomatoes, seeded and chopped

3 tablespoons balsamic vinegar

2 teaspoons olive oil

2 teaspoons firmly packed brown sugar

¾ teaspoon dried tarragon

½ teaspoon salt

¼ teaspoon freshly ground black pepper

½ cup chopped fresh basil or mint

⅓ cup grated Parmesan cheese

1. In a large pot of boiling water, cook the garlic for 2 minutes to blanch. With a slotted spoon, transfer the garlic to a cutting board and mince. Add the spaghetti to the boiling water and cook until just tender.

2. Meanwhile, in a large bowl, combine the garlic and the tomatoes. Add the vinegar, oil, sugar, tarragon, salt, and pepper, stirring to combine. When the pasta is done, drain and transfer to the bowl with the tomato mixture. Add the basil and Parmesan and toss well. Divide among 4 bowls and serve.

Helpful hint: Other long pastas, such as perciatelli (thick, hollow spaghetti), vermicelli, linguine, or fettuccine can be substituted for the spaghetti.

FAT: 6G/13%
CALORIES: 426
SATURATED FAT: 1.8G
CARBOHYDRATE: 77G
PROTEIN: 16G
CHOLESTEROL: 5MG
SODIUM: 423MG

ZITI WITH SPICY PORK AND TOMATO SAUCE

SERVES: 4
WORKING TIME: 25 MINUTES
TOTAL TIME: 25 MINUTES

12 ounces ziti pasta

2 teaspoons olive oil

3 cloves garlic, minced

¾ cup chopped celery

1 teaspoon fennel seeds

6 ounces well-trimmed pork tenderloin, cut into ¼-inch thick slivers

¾ cup reduced-sodium chicken broth, defatted

¼ cup dry white wine

1 tablespoon cornstarch mixed with 1 tablespoon water

1 pound plum tomatoes, diced

¼ cup golden raisins

½ teaspoon hot pepper sauce

1 teaspoon salt

¾ teaspoon dried oregano

½ teaspoon paprika

2 tablespoons grated Parmesan cheese

1. In a large pot of boiling water, cook the ziti until just tender. Drain well.

2. Meanwhile, in a large saucepan, heat the oil until hot but not smoking over medium heat. Add the garlic, celery, and fennel seeds and cook until the celery is softened, about 8 minutes. Add the pork to the pan and cook until the pork is no longer pink, about 1 minute.

3. In a small bowl, combine the broth, wine, and cornstarch mixture. Add the broth-cornstarch mixture, the tomatoes, raisins, hot pepper sauce, salt, oregano, and paprika to the saucepan. Bring to a boil and cook until the pork is cooked through and the sauce is slightly thickened, about 1 minute.

4. Add the cooked ziti to the saucepan, tossing to coat well with the sauce. Divide the pasta among 4 plates, sprinkle with the Parmesan, and serve.

Helpful hint: If you're fond of fennel, substitute it for the celery; the fennel seeds will further accentuate its flavor.

FAT: 6G/11%
CALORIES: 480
SATURATED FAT: 1.5G
CARBOHYDRATE: 80G
PROTEIN: 23G
CHOLESTEROL: 30MG
SODIUM: 794MG

S atisfy winter appetites with this hearty and well-seasoned "unbaked" ziti—it's made in a skillet on the stovetop.

Fresh Fettuccine with Tomato Cream Sauce

SERVES: 4
WORKING TIME: 20 MINUTES
TOTAL TIME: 30 MINUTES

*1 red bell pepper, halved
lengthwise and seeded*

1 cup evaporated low-fat milk

¼ cup grated Parmesan cheese

½ teaspoon salt

*½ teaspoon freshly ground black
pepper*

1 teaspoon olive oil

*3 tablespoons finely chopped
prosciutto or Canadian bacon
(1 ounce)*

*2 cups canned no-salt-added
tomatoes, coarsely chopped with
their juices*

1 cup frozen peas, thawed

1 pound fresh fettuccine

1. Preheat the broiler. Place the bell pepper halves, cut-sides down, on the broiler rack. Broil the pepper 4 inches from the heat for 10 minutes, or until the skin is blackened. When the peppers are cool enough to handle, peel them and cut into thin strips. Start heating a large pot of water to boiling for the pasta.

2. Meanwhile, in a large bowl, combine the evaporated milk, Parmesan, salt, and pepper. Set aside.

3. In a large nonstick skillet, heat the oil until hot but not smoking over medium heat. Add the prosciutto and cook until lightly crisped, about 2 minutes. Add the tomatoes and red pepper strips and cook, stirring occasionally, until flavorful and lightly thickened, about 5 minutes. Add the peas and cook until heated through, about 2 minutes.

4. Cook the fettuccine in the boiling water until just tender. Drain and add to the milk and Parmesan mixture, tossing well to coat and to melt the cheese. Transfer the pasta to the tomato sauce in the skillet, toss to coat, and serve.

Helpful hint: You can substitute 12 ounces of dried fettuccine for the fresh pasta.

FAT: 10G/15%
CALORIES: 593
SATURATED FAT: 2.4G
CARBOHYDRATE: 98G
PROTEIN: 28G
CHOLESTEROL: 128MG
SODIUM: 823MG

The "cream" in this recipe is really evaporated low-fat milk. Here are the impressive figures on this "miracle" ingredient: Evaporated low-fat milk has a mere 3 grams of fat per cup, while the same amount of heavy cream has a whopping 90 grams! It's one of the more dramatic ways to cut fat in a sauce without sacrificing luxurious richness.

Long Fusilli with Porcini and Chicken

SERVES: 4
WORKING TIME: 35 MINUTES
TOTAL TIME: 40 MINUTES

Porcini mushrooms are pricier than other dried mushrooms, but you'll find that a small amount goes a long way. Instead of whole dried porcini, you can buy a bag of small dried mushroom pieces, which are quite reasonably priced. Follow this fragrant pasta entrée with a refreshing dessert of citrus fruit—oranges, tangerines, or, for a more exotic touch, kumquats.

½ ounce dried mushrooms, preferably porcini

1 cup boiling water

2 teaspoons olive oil

1 large onion, finely chopped

3 cloves garlic, minced

1 large carrot, finely chopped

1 cup reduced-sodium chicken broth, defatted

½ pound skinless, boneless chicken thighs, cut into ½-inch pieces

¼ cup no-salt-added tomato paste

½ teaspoon dried rosemary

½ teaspoon salt

¼ teaspoon freshly ground black pepper

10 ounces long fusilli

3 tablespoons grated Parmesan cheese

1. In a small bowl, combine the dried mushrooms and boiling water and let stand until the mushrooms have softened, about 10 minutes. Scoop the dried mushrooms from their soaking liquid, reserving the liquid, then rinse and coarsely chop the mushrooms. Strain the liquid through a paper towel-lined sieve and set aside.

2. Meanwhile, in a large nonstick skillet, heat the oil until hot but not smoking over medium heat. Add the onion and garlic and cook, stirring occasionally, until the onion is softened, about 7 minutes. Add the carrot and ¼ cup of the broth and cook, stirring frequently, until softened, about 5 minutes.

3. Add the chicken, stirring to coat. Add the tomato paste, mushrooms, the reserved soaking liquid, the remaining ¾ cup broth, the rosemary, salt, and pepper and bring to a boil. Reduce to a simmer and cook until the sauce is slightly thickened and the chicken is cooked through, about 5 minutes.

4. Meanwhile, in a large pot of boiling water, cook the fusilli until just tender. Drain well. Transfer the pasta to a large bowl, add the sauce, and toss to combine. Add the Parmesan, toss again, spoon into 4 pasta bowls, and serve.

Helpful hint: Seal dried mushrooms in a plastic bag (their aroma is quite powerful), and store them in the freezer.

FAT: 7G/15%
CALORIES: 432
SATURATED FAT: 1.8G
CARBOHYDRATE: 67G
PROTEIN: 25G
CHOLESTEROL: 50MG
SODIUM: 581MG

CHEESE TORTELLINI WITH PROSCIUTTO AND PEAS

SERVES: 4
WORKING TIME: 20 MINUTES
TOTAL TIME: 50 MINUTES

Keep
*a package of fresh
cheese tortellini on
hand and you'll be
ready to make this
great meal on short
notice.*

1 teaspoon olive oil

1 onion, coarsely chopped

2 cloves garlic, minced

2 cups sliced mushrooms

¼ teaspoon red pepper flakes

Two 16-ounce cans no-salt-
added tomatoes, drained and
chopped

⅓ cup dry red wine

⅓ cup chopped fresh basil

¼ cup plus 2 tablespoons finely
chopped prosciutto or
Canadian bacon (2 ounces)

2 cups frozen peas, thawed

15-ounce package fresh cheese
tortellini

1. In a large nonstick saucepan, heat the oil until hot but not smoking over medium heat. Add the onion and cook until softened, about 5 minutes. Add the garlic, mushrooms, and red pepper flakes and cook, stirring, until the mushrooms are tender, about 5 minutes.

2. Add the tomatoes and wine, bring to simmer, and cook until slightly thickened, about 15 minutes. Stir in the basil, prosciutto, and peas and cook until the peas are warmed through, about 2 minutes.

3. Meanwhile, in a large pot of boiling water, cook the tortellini until just tender. Drain well. Toss the tortellini with the sauce, divide among 4 bowls, and serve.

Helpful hint: If you have a hinged egg slicer, you can use it to slice mushrooms quickly. Buy large mushrooms and place them stemmed-side up in the slicer.

FAT: 12G/21%
CALORIES: 508
SATURATED FAT: 3.9G
CARBOHYDRATE: 77G
PROTEIN: 25G
CHOLESTEROL: 55MG
SODIUM: 736MG

POULTRY, MEAT & SEAFOOD

3

Herbed Stuffed Swordfish

SERVES: 4
WORKING TIME: 25 MINUTES
TOTAL TIME: 30 MINUTES

The dense flesh of swordfish (pesce spada in Italian) can actually be pounded like veal scallopini. And the flavor of swordfish is robust enough to be partnered with a tangy, aromatic mixture of marmalade, rosemary, oregano, and red wine vinegar. A salad made with arugula, which has a uniquely assertive flavor of its own, rounds out the meal.

½ cup chopped fresh parsley
¼ cup plain dried bread crumbs
½ teaspoon grated orange zest
½ teaspoon dried oregano
½ teaspoon dried rosemary
¾ teaspoon salt
4 swordfish steaks, cut ½ inch thick (about 1¼ pounds total)
½ cup orange juice
2 tablespoons orange marmalade
2 tablespoons red wine vinegar
2 teaspoons extra-virgin olive oil
½ cup finely diced jarred roasted red pepper
1 small red onion, finely diced
1 rib celery, finely diced

1. Preheat the oven to 400°. Spray a 9-inch square baking dish with nonstick cooking spray.

2. In a small bowl, combine ¼ cup of the parsley, the bread crumbs, orange zest, oregano, rosemary, and ½ teaspoon of the salt.

3. Place the swordfish steaks between 2 sheets of waxed paper and, with the flat side of a small skillet or meat pounder, pound the swordfish to a ¼-inch thickness. Lay the swordfish flat and sprinkle with ¼ cup of the orange juice. Spoon the parsley mixture over the fish and, starting from a short side, neatly roll up each piece. Place the fish, seam-side down, in the prepared baking dish, cover with foil, and bake for 7 minutes, or until the rolls are just opaque in the center.

4. Meanwhile, in a medium bowl, combine the remaining ¼ cup orange juice, the marmalade, vinegar, oil, red pepper, onion, celery, the remaining ¼ cup parsley, and the remaining ¼ teaspoon salt. Place the fish rolls on 4 plates, spoon the sauce on top, and serve.

Helpful hint: Although meat pounders come in various shapes—some look like mallets, others like long-stemmed mushrooms—their one essential quality is weight.

FAT: 8G/27%
CALORIES: 263
SATURATED FAT: 1.8G
CARBOHYDRATE: 20G
PROTEIN: 27G
CHOLESTEROL: 49MG
SODIUM: 640MG

In Italian, "saltimbocca" means something that leaps into the mouth— an apt description for these prosciutto-and-sage-filled chicken bundles. This Roman specialty is usually made with veal, but chicken breasts are a perfectly delicious and low-fat substitute. Serve colorful steamed carrot and zucchini sticks on the side.

CHICKEN SALTIMBOCCA

Serves: 4
Working time: 30 minutes
Total time: 30 minutes

4 chicken cutlets (about
1 pound total)

¼ teaspoon salt

⅛ teaspoon freshly ground black
pepper

¼ ounce prosciutto, cut into
¼-inch-wide strips, or ¼ ounce
Canadian bacon, cut into very
thin slivers

6 fresh sage leaves, slivered, or
½ teaspoon dried sage

1 teaspoon olive oil

1 shallot or scallion, finely
chopped

¼ cup dry white wine

¼ cup reduced-sodium chicken
broth, defatted

1 teaspoon cornstarch

1 tablespoon fresh lemon juice

1. Sprinkle the chicken with the salt and pepper. Place the cutlets on a work surface and sprinkle the prosciutto crosswise along the center of the cutlets. Fold one-third of the chicken on top of itself (see tip) and sprinkle with the sage. Fold the remaining third of the chicken over.

2. In a large nonstick skillet, heat the oil until hot but not smoking over medium heat. Add the chicken, seam-sides down, and cook until golden, about 3 minutes per side. Push the chicken to one side of the pan, add the shallot, and cook for 1 minute to soften.

3. Meanwhile, in a small bowl, combine the wine, broth, cornstarch, and lemon juice and add to the pan, stirring constantly. Bring to a boil and cook for 1 minute. Cook, covered, until the chicken is cooked through, about 3 minutes. Place the chicken and sauce on a platter and serve.

Helpful hints: When you bring home fresh sage, wrap the leaves in a paper towel, then slip them into a plastic bag and store in the refrigerator for up to 1 week. To make your own chicken cutlets: Buy 4 skinless, boneless chicken breast halves (about 1 pound total). Place each breast half between 2 sheets of waxed paper and, with the flat side of a small skillet or meat pounder, pound the breast half to a ¼-inch thickness.

Fat: 3g/17%
Calories: 156
Saturated Fat: .6g
Carbohydrate: 2g
Protein: 27g
Cholesterol: 67mg
Sodium: 283mg

After sprinkling prosciutto down the center of a chicken cutlet, fold one-third of the cutlet in toward the center to cover the prosciutto. Sprinkle the sage over the chicken before folding over the remaining third of the cutlet to make a compact bundle.

SAUTÉED PORK SCALLOPINI ON A BED OF GREENS

SERVES: 4
WORKING TIME: 20 MINUTES
TOTAL TIME: 25 MINUTES

1¼ pounds small red potatoes, quartered

¾ teaspoon salt

2 tablespoons balsamic vinegar

2 teaspoons olive oil

1 teaspoon Dijon mustard

¾ teaspoon firmly packed brown sugar

½ teaspoon freshly ground black pepper

2 cups watercress or arugula leaves

2 tomatoes, cut into small wedges

1 Belgian endive, cut into 1-inch pieces, or 2 cups torn Boston lettuce

¾ pound well-trimmed center-cut pork loin, cut into 8 slices

2 tablespoons flour

1. In a large pot of boiling water, cook the potatoes with ¼ teaspoon of the salt until tender, about 15 minutes. Drain well.

2. Meanwhile, in a large bowl, combine the vinegar, 1 teaspoon of the oil, the mustard, brown sugar, ¼ teaspoon of the remaining salt, and ¼ teaspoon of the pepper. Place the watercress, tomatoes, and endive on top of the dressing, but do not toss. When the potatoes are done, add them to the salad. Set aside.

3. Place the pork slices between 2 sheets of waxed paper, and with the flat side of a small skillet or meat pounder, pound the pork to a ¼-inch thickness. On another sheet of waxed paper, combine the flour, the remaining ¼ teaspoon salt, and the remaining ¼ teaspoon pepper. Dredge the pork in the flour mixture, shaking off the excess.

4. In a large nonstick skillet, heat the remaining 1 teaspoon oil until hot but not smoking over medium-high heat. Add the pork and cook until browned and cooked through, about 2 minutes per side. Toss the salad mixture together, spoon onto 4 plates, top with the pork cutlets, and serve.

Helpful hint: Belgian endive discolors and turns bitter when exposed to light, so it's wrapped in paper within its shipping box. When shopping for Belgian endive, dig to the bottom of the box for small, pale heads that have been protected from the light.

FAT: 7G/22%
CALORIES: 291
SATURATED FAT: 1.8G
CARBOHYDRATE: 33G
PROTEIN: 23G
CHOLESTEROL: 54MG
SODIUM: 457MG

7 4

For this innovative one-dish meal, tender pork cutlets are served on a warm potato-and-greens salad. The slight bitterness of the watercress and endive is balanced by the delicate sweetness of the mustard and brown sugar vinaigrette. Serve this satisfying entrée with a basket of Italian bread.

SHRIMP ALL'ARRABBIATA

SERVES: 4
WORKING TIME: 25 MINUTES
TOTAL TIME: 25 MINUTES

In Italian, arrabbiata means "angry," and appropriately, the shrimp in this dish are bathed in a fiery tomato sauce. The sauce, seasoned with red pepper flakes, oregano, ginger, and rosemary, is brightened with bits of bell pepper and olives. For a colorful side dish, toss together a salad of radicchio, baby spinach, and other tender greens.

1 teaspoon olive oil
1 red bell pepper, diced
2 cloves garlic, minced
¾ cup bottled clam juice
1 tomato, chopped
¼ cup Calamata or other brine-cured black olives, pitted and slivered
¾ teaspoon dried oregano
½ teaspoon ground ginger
½ teaspoon dried rosemary
¼ teaspoon red pepper flakes
¼ teaspoon salt
1 pound medium shrimp, shelled and deveined
¾ teaspoon cornstarch mixed with 1 teaspoon water

1. In a large nonstick skillet, heat the oil until hot but not smoking over medium heat. Add the bell pepper and garlic and cook, stirring, until well coated, about 1 minute. Add ¼ cup of the clam juice and cook until the pepper is softened, about 3 minutes. Stir in the remaining ½ cup clam juice, the tomato, olives, oregano, ginger, rosemary, red pepper flakes, and salt and cook for 3 minutes to reduce slightly.

2. Add the shrimp to the pan and cook until the shrimp are just opaque, about 2 minutes. Bring to a boil, stir in the cornstarch mixture, and cook, stirring, until slightly thickened, about 1 minute. Divide the shrimp mixture among 4 plates and serve.

Helpful hint: Clam juice is ideal for seafood sauces, but you can substitute chicken broth if necessary.

FAT: 4G/26%
CALORIES: 139
SATURATED FAT: .6G
CARBOHYDRATE: 5G
PROTEIN: 19G
CHOLESTEROL: 140MG
SODIUM: 448MG

BROILED FLORENTINE STEAK WITH CANNELLINI

SERVES: 4
WORKING TIME: 35 MINUTES
TOTAL TIME: 50 MINUTES

This variation on "bistecca alla fiorentina" pays homage to both Florence and Tuscany, a region famed for its fine beef.

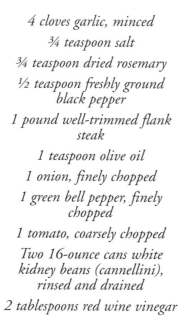

4 cloves garlic, minced

¾ teaspoon salt

¾ teaspoon dried rosemary

½ teaspoon freshly ground black pepper

1 pound well-trimmed flank steak

1 teaspoon olive oil

1 onion, finely chopped

1 green bell pepper, finely chopped

1 tomato, coarsely chopped

Two 16-ounce cans white kidney beans (cannellini), rinsed and drained

2 tablespoons red wine vinegar

1. Sprinkle half of the garlic, ½ teaspoon of the salt, ½ teaspoon of the rosemary, and the black pepper on the flank steak and rub it in. Let stand at room temperature while you cook the beans.

2. In a large nonstick skillet, heat the oil until hot but not smoking over medium heat. Add the onion and the remaining garlic and cook, stirring frequently, until the onion is softened, about 7 minutes. Add the bell pepper, stirring to coat. Stir in the tomato, the remaining ¼ teaspoon salt, and remaining ¼ teaspoon rosemary and cook, stirring frequently, until the mixture is slightly thickened, about 5 minutes. Stir in the beans, ¼ cup of water, and the vinegar, reduce the heat to low, cover, and cook, stirring occasionally, until the beans are richly flavored, about 5 minutes.

3. Preheat the broiler or prepare the grill. Broil or grill the beef 6 inches from the heat, turning once, for 8 minutes, or until medium-rare. Let stand for 5 minutes, then cut into thin diagonal slices. Divide the steak among 4 plates, spoon the beans alongside, and serve.

Helpful hint: You can substitute pink or red kidney beans for the cannellini if you like.

FAT: 11G/26%
CALORIES: 381
SATURATED FAT: 4G
CARBOHYDRATE: 33G
PROTEIN: 36G
CHOLESTEROL: 57MG
SODIUM: 769MG

Pork Chops with Basil and Peppers

Serves: 4
Working time: 20 minutes
Total time: 35 minutes

1 cup long-grain rice

¾ teaspoon salt

2 tablespoons flour

½ teaspoon freshly ground black pepper

4 well-trimmed center-cut pork loin chops (about 1 pound total)

2 teaspoons olive oil

1 red bell pepper, thinly sliced

1 green bell pepper, thinly sliced

¾ cup dry vermouth or dry white wine

2 cloves garlic, thinly sliced

1 tomato, coarsely chopped

¼ cup chopped fresh basil

2 tablespoons no-salt-added tomato paste

1 tablespoon capers, rinsed and drained

1. In a medium saucepan, bring 2¼ cups of water to a boil. Add the rice and ¼ teaspoon of the salt, reduce to a simmer, cover, and cook until the rice is tender, about 17 minutes.

2. Meanwhile, on a sheet of waxed paper, combine the flour, ¼ teaspoon of the remaining salt, and ¼ teaspoon of the black pepper. Dredge the pork in the flour mixture, shaking off the excess.

3. In a large nonstick skillet, heat the oil until hot but not smoking over medium-high heat. Add the pork chops and cook until golden brown and almost cooked through, about 2 minutes per side. With a spatula, transfer the pork chops to a plate.

4. Reduce the heat to medium. Add the bell peppers, stirring to coat. Add the vermouth and garlic and cook until the peppers are tender, about 5 minutes. Add the tomato, basil, tomato paste, capers, ¼ cup of water, the remaining ¼ teaspoon salt, and the remaining ¼ teaspoon black pepper. Cover and cook, stirring frequently, until the sauce is richly flavored and glossy, about 6 minutes. Reduce the heat to low, return the pork chops to the pan, cover, and cook just until the chops are cooked through, about 2 minutes. Place the pork chops, peppers, and rice on 4 plates and serve.

Helpful hint: Vermouth is a fortified wine enhanced with herbs, spices, and other flavorings. White wine may be substituted.

Fat: 7g/16%
Calories: 400
Saturated Fat: 1.8g
Carbohydrate: 49g
Protein: 22g
Cholesterol: 50mg
Sodium: 535mg

A*n Italian peperonata (braised peppers and tomatoes) sauces these pork chops. Serve them with steamed rice.*

79

CHICKEN WITH HONEY-WALNUT SAUCE

SERVES: 4
WORKING TIME: 20 MINUTES
TOTAL TIME: 35 MINUTES

Although most of Italy's walnuts grow in the south, they're more prevalent in northern cuisine, as seen in the Milanese recipe for roast chicken stuffed with walnuts and in this Ligurian walnut sauce for pasta, among others. Here, broiled chicken breasts are sauced with a tangy-sweet mixture of walnuts, honey, and mustard. Sautéed yellow squash with scallions is a nice light side dish.

2 cloves garlic, peeled
⅓ cup chopped fresh parsley
1 teaspoon grated lemon zest
3 tablespoons fresh lemon juice
2 teaspoons olive oil
½ teaspoon salt
½ teaspoon dried rosemary
4 skinless, boneless chicken breast halves (about 1 pound total)
3 tablespoons honey
3 tablespoons reduced-sodium chicken broth, defatted
2 tablespoons finely chopped walnuts
1 tablespoon Dijon mustard

1. In a small pot of boiling water, cook the garlic for 2 minutes to blanch. Drain and finely chop. In a small bowl, combine the garlic, parsley, and lemon zest. Set aside.

2. Preheat the broiler or prepare the grill. In a large bowl, combine 2 tablespoons of the lemon juice, the oil, salt, and rosemary. Add the chicken, turning to coat well. Place the chicken on the broiler rack and broil or grill 6 inches from the heat, turning once, for 8 minutes, or until golden brown and cooked through.

3. Meanwhile, in a small bowl, combine the honey, broth, walnuts, mustard, and the remaining 1 tablespoon lemon juice. Place the chicken on 4 plates, spoon the sauce over the chicken, sprinkle with the parsley mixture, and serve.

Helpful hint: Walnuts (all nuts, in fact) are quite high in fat and therefore have the potential to become rancid. Store them in a tightly closed bag in the refrigerator or freezer.

FAT: 6G/24%
CALORIES: 229
SATURATED FAT: .9G
CARBOHYDRATE: 16G
PROTEIN: 27G
CHOLESTEROL: 66MG
SODIUM: 471MG

STEAK WITH CHUNKY TOMATO SAUCE AND POTATOES

SERVES: 4
WORKING TIME: 40 MINUTES
TOTAL TIME: 45 MINUTES

Hold the ketchup! No need to sully steaks with something from a bottle when you can savor this fresh, summery tomato sauce, enlivened with bits of carrot, onion, and garlic. The steaks and sauce cook while you boil the accompanying potatoes. Serve a simple salad, too, and put a pinch of oregano in the dressing to complement the sauce.

1 pound all-purpose potatoes, peeled and cut into 1-inch cubes

¼ cup chopped fresh parsley

1 tablespoon extra-virgin olive oil

½ teaspoon salt

1 large onion, finely chopped

2 cloves garlic, minced

¾ cup reduced-sodium chicken broth, defatted

1 carrot, finely chopped

2 tomatoes, coarsely chopped

½ teaspoon dried oregano

½ teaspoon dried rosemary

1 pound well-trimmed top round of beef, cut into 4 thin steaks

1. In a large pot of boiling water, cook the potatoes until tender, about 15 minutes. Drain well and toss with the parsley, ½ teaspoon of the oil, and ¼ teaspoon of the salt. Set aside.

2. In a large nonstick skillet, heat 1 teaspoon of the remaining oil until hot but not smoking over medium heat. Add the onion and garlic and stir to coat. Add ¼ cup of the broth and cook, stirring frequently, until the onion is softened, about 5 minutes. Add the carrot and cook, stirring frequently, until the carrot is softened, about 4 minutes. Stir in the remaining ½ cup broth and cook until slightly reduced, about 4 minutes. Stir in the tomatoes, oregano, and rosemary and cook until the sauce is slightly reduced, about 5 minutes.

3. Meanwhile, in another large nonstick skillet, heat the remaining 1½ teaspoons oil until hot but not smoking over medium-high heat. Sprinkle the steaks with the remaining ¼ teaspoon salt and cook until lightly browned and just cooked through, about 2 minutes per side. Place the steaks and potatoes on 4 plates, spoon the sauce over the steaks, and serve.

Helpful hint: Tan-skinned "long white" all-purpose potatoes are good for boiling; don't confuse them with "long russets"—baking potatoes—which are starchier and will fall apart if peeled and boiled.

FAT: 10G/29%
CALORIES: 304
SATURATED FAT: 2.4G
CARBOHYDRATE: 26G
PROTEIN: 29G
CHOLESTEROL: 66MG
SODIUM: 479MG

This traditional Tuscan method for cooking game birds such as quail and squab is called "al mattone" (with bricks); special heavy clay tiles are commonly used to weight the birds in the pan. A layer of foil plus a heavy skillet or pot lid placed on these hens serves the same purpose: The birds brown beautifully, emerging with a glorious golden finish.

PAN-ROASTED GAME HENS WITH SAGE AND GARLIC

SERVES: 4
WORKING TIME: 20 MINUTES
TOTAL TIME: 50 MINUTES

2 tablespoons fresh lemon juice

3 cloves garlic, minced

12 fresh sage leaves or
¾ teaspoon dried sage

½ teaspoon salt

½ teaspoon freshly ground black
pepper

2 Cornish game hens
(1½ pounds each), skinned and
quartered

2 teaspoons olive oil

1 pound all-purpose potatoes,
peeled and thinly sliced

¾ cup reduced-sodium chicken
broth, defatted

⅔ cup dry white wine

1. In a large bowl, combine the lemon juice, garlic, sage, ¼ teaspoon of the salt, and the pepper. Add the hen pieces, tossing to coat. Set aside.

2. In a skillet or Dutch oven large enough to hold the hens in a single layer, heat the oil until hot but not smoking over medium heat. Place the hen pieces, skinned-sides down, in the pan and drizzle with the marinade. Place a piece of foil over the hens to loosely cover. Place a smaller, heavy metal pan or lid over the foil (see tip). Cook until the hens are golden brown, about 10 minutes.

3. Meanwhile, in a large pot of boiling water, cook the potatoes with the remaining ¼ teaspoon salt until the potatoes are almost tender, about 10 minutes. Drain.

4. Remove the small, heavy pan and the foil. Pour the broth and wine into the pan, bring to a boil, and cook for 1 minute. Reduce the heat to a simmer, transfer the hen pieces to a plate, and set aside. Add the potatoes to the skillet, stirring to coat. Return the hen pieces to the skillet, arranging them, skinned-sides-up, on top of the potatoes. Cook, uncovered, until the potatoes and hens are cooked through, about 15 minutes.

FAT: 7G/20%
CALORIES: 318
SATURATED FAT: 1.6G
CARBOHYDRATE: 18G
PROTEIN: 38G
CHOLESTEROL: 114MG
SODIUM: 528MG

TIP

A weight placed on top of the Cornish hens keeps them pressed against the hot surface of the skillet as they cook, thus turning the hens a deep golden color. The effect is similar to that of using a spatula to press a hamburger down as it cooks—but this method leaves the cook free to attend to other matters in the kitchen. Foil is placed on the hens first to keep in moisture and prevent the hens from drying out.

COD AGRODOLCE WITH MINT

SERVES: 4
WORKING TIME: 40 MINUTES
TOTAL TIME: 45 MINUTES

⅓ cup raisins

¾ cup boiling water

2 tablespoons flour

½ teaspoon salt

½ teaspoon freshly ground black pepper

4 cod fillets, any visible bones removed (about 1½ pounds total)

4 teaspoons olive oil

2 large onions, halved and thinly sliced

2 teaspoons sugar

½ cup dry red wine

⅓ cup red wine vinegar or balsamic vinegar

2 tablespoons no-salt-added tomato paste

¼ cup chopped fresh mint

1. In a small bowl, combine the raisins and water. Set aside to soften.

2. On a sheet of waxed paper, combine the flour, ¼ teaspoon of the salt, and ¼ teaspoon of the pepper. Dredge the cod in the flour mixture, shaking off the excess. In a large nonstick skillet, heat 2 teaspoons of the oil until hot but not smoking over medium-high heat. Add the cod and cook until golden brown and cooked through, about 3 minutes per side. With a spatula, transfer the cod to a plate.

3. Add the remaining 2 teaspoons oil and the onions to the skillet, stirring to coat. Sprinkle the sugar on top and cook, stirring frequently, until the onions are golden brown, about 10 minutes. Add the wine and boil for 2 minutes. Add the vinegar, tomato paste, the raisins and their soaking liquid, the remaining ¼ teaspoon salt, and remaining ¼ teaspoon pepper and cook until the sauce is slightly thickened, about 5 minutes. Place the fish on 4 plates, top with the sauce, sprinkle with the mint, and serve.

Helpful hint: This dish actually improves with age, so it can be made well ahead of serving. After cooking the fish, place it in a shallow container, top with the sauce, and let stand for 1 hour at room temperature or for up to 12 hours in the refrigerator. The fish can be served hot, chilled, or at room temperature.

FAT: 6G/17%
CALORIES: 313
SATURATED FAT: .9G
CARBOHYDRATE: 27G
PROTEIN: 33G
CHOLESTEROL: 73MG
SODIUM: 377MG

This dish has ancient roots that historians trace back to the Near East. "Agrodolce" means sweet-and-sour in Italian; the sauce may be made with honey or sugar combined with lemon juice or vinegar. Here, onions and raisins are braised to make a sweet topping for the fish; red wine vinegar provides the "sour." Round out the meal with steamed green beans and a loaf of peasant bread.

GRILLED CHICKEN WITH SALSA VERDE

SERVES: 4
WORKING TIME: 20 MINUTES
TOTAL TIME: 35 MINUTES

A traditional accompaniment for bollito misto—a lavish meal of a dozen or more different meats— is salsa verde, a piquant green herb sauce. In this dish, a lighter version of the classic sauce is thickened with mashed potatoes rather than with copious quantities of olive oil and is served alongside a simple herb-marinated broiled chicken.

⅓ cup fresh lemon juice
¼ cup chopped fresh basil
¾ teaspoon dried oregano,
2 cloves garlic, minced
4 skinless, boneless chicken breast halves (about 1 pound total)
½ pound all-purpose potatoes, peeled and thinly sliced
½ cup reduced-sodium chicken broth, defatted
⅓ cup chopped fresh parsley
¼ cup gherkins, finely chopped
1 tablespoon capers, rinsed and drained
1 tablespoon extra-virgin olive oil

1. In a large bowl, combine 2 tablespoons of the lemon juice, the basil, oregano, and garlic. Add the chicken, turning to coat well. Set aside to marinate while you make the sauce and preheat the broiler.

2. Preheat the broiler or prepare the grill. In a large pot of boiling water, cook the potatoes until tender, about 10 minutes. Drain well. Place the potatoes in a medium bowl and mash. Add the broth, parsley, gherkins, capers, oil, and the remaining lemon juice, whisking until well combined.

3. Broil or grill the chicken 6 inches from the heat, turning once, for 8 minutes, or until golden brown and cooked through. Place the chicken on 4 plates, spoon the sauce over, and serve.

Helpful hint: When you're using parsley more for flavor than for looks, as in this case, choose the Italian flat-leaf rather than the curly type.

FAT: 5G/20%
CALORIES: 225
SATURATED FAT: .9G
CARBOHYDRATE: 17G
PROTEIN: 28G
CHOLESTEROL: 66MG
SODIUM: 324MG

STEAK WITH BALSAMIC SAUCE AND MUSHROOMS

SERVES: 4
WORKING TIME: 15 MINUTES
TOTAL TIME: 30 MINUTES PLUS MARINATING TIME

A

citrus-and-vinegar marinade suffuses this steak with flavor. Serve the steak with sautéed broccoli rabe.

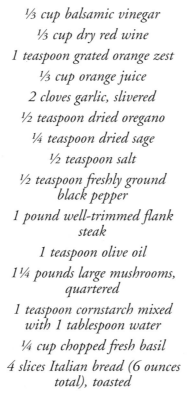

⅓ cup balsamic vinegar

⅓ cup dry red wine

1 teaspoon grated orange zest

⅓ cup orange juice

2 cloves garlic, slivered

½ teaspoon dried oregano

¼ teaspoon dried sage

½ teaspoon salt

½ teaspoon freshly ground black pepper

1 pound well-trimmed flank steak

1 teaspoon olive oil

1¼ pounds large mushrooms, quartered

1 teaspoon cornstarch mixed with 1 tablespoon water

¼ cup chopped fresh basil

4 slices Italian bread (6 ounces total), toasted

1. In a shallow nonaluminum pan or bowl, combine the vinegar, wine, orange zest, orange juice, garlic, oregano, sage, salt, and pepper. Add the steak, turning to coat. Set aside to marinate for at least 30 minutes at room temperature or for up to 8 hours in the refrigerator.

2. Preheat the broiler or prepare the grill. Reserving the marinade, place the steak on the rack and broil or grill 6 inches from the heat, turning once, for 8 minutes, or until medium-rare. Let stand for 5 minutes before cutting into thin diagonal slices.

3. Meanwhile, in a large nonstick skillet, heat the oil until hot but not smoking over medium heat. Add the mushrooms and cook, stirring frequently, until softened, about 4 minutes. Pour in the reserved marinade and bring to a boil. Boil until reduced by one-fourth, about 5 minutes. Stir in the cornstarch mixture and cook, stirring, until slightly thickened, about 1 minute. Stir the basil into the pan. Place the steak, mushrooms, and toasted bread on 4 plates and serve.

Helpful hint: Try handsome light-brown cremini mushrooms in this dish if you can find them; they have a little more flavor than domestic white mushrooms. Many supermarkets now carry these Italian mushrooms.

FAT: 12G/29%
CALORIES: 372
SATURATED FAT: 4.3G
CARBOHYDRATE: 33G
PROTEIN: 30G
CHOLESTEROL: 57MG
SODIUM: 601MG

PORK CUTLETS IN BASIL AND RED WINE SAUCE

SERVES: 4
WORKING TIME: 30 MINUTES
TOTAL TIME: 30 MINUTES

8 ounces orzo

¼ cup chopped fresh basil

¾ pound well-trimmed center-cut pork loin, cut into 8 slices

2 tablespoons flour

¾ teaspoon salt

½ teaspoon freshly ground black pepper

2 teaspoons olive oil

½ cup dry red wine

¾ cup reduced-sodium chicken broth, defatted

1 tablespoon fresh lemon juice

⅔ cup frozen peas

1 teaspoon cornstarch mixed with 1 tablespoon water

1. In a large pot of boiling water, cook the orzo until just tender. Drain well, transfer to a medium bowl, and toss with 1 tablespoon of the basil.

2. Meanwhile, place the pork slices between two sheets of waxed paper, and with the flat side of a small skillet or meat pounder, pound the pork to a ¼-inch thickness. On another sheet of waxed paper, combine the flour, ¼ teaspoon of the salt, and ¼ teaspoon of the pepper. Dredge the pork in the flour mixture, shaking off the excess. In a large nonstick skillet, heat the oil until hot but not smoking over medium-high heat. Add the pork and cook until golden brown and cooked through, about 2 minutes per side. With a spatula, transfer the pork to a plate.

3. Add the wine to the pan, stirring to scrape up any browned bits that cling to the bottom of the pan, and cook for 2 minutes. Add the broth, lemon juice, the remaining ½ teaspoon salt, and remaining ¼ teaspoon pepper and cook until slightly reduced, about 2 minutes. Stir in the peas and bring to a boil. Stir in the cornstarch mixture and cook, stirring, until slightly thickened, about 1 minute. Stir in 2 tablespoons of the remaining basil. Place the pork on 4 plates, top with the sauce, and sprinkle with the remaining 1 tablespoon basil. Spoon the orzo alongside and serve.

FAT: 8G/17%
CALORIES: 414
SATURATED FAT: 1.9G
CARBOHYDRATE: 51G
PROTEIN: 29G
CHOLESTEROL: 54MG
SODIUM: 622MG

Pork, cooked in the manner of scallopini, is dressed up with wine sauce and peas here and served with orzo.

CHICKEN BOLOGNESE

SERVES: 4
WORKING TIME: 30 MINUTES
TOTAL TIME: 40 MINUTES

4 skinless, boneless chicken breasts halves (about 1 pound total)

¼ cup flour

½ teaspoon salt

⅛ teaspoon freshly ground black pepper

2 teaspoons olive oil

1 pound plum tomatoes, coarsely chopped

¾ pound small red potatoes, cut into ¾-inch cubes

2 cups sliced mushrooms

1½ tablespoons chopped prosciutto or Canadian bacon (½ ounce)

½ cup reduced-sodium chicken broth, defatted

¼ cup dry white wine

2 cloves garlic, minced

1 tablespoon chopped fresh rosemary or ½ teaspoon dried

1. Place the chicken between 2 sheets of waxed paper and, with the flat side of a small skillet or meat pounder, flatten the chicken to a ¼-inch thickness. On another sheet of waxed paper, combine the flour, ¼ teaspoon of the salt, and the pepper. Dredge the chicken in the flour mixture, shaking off and reserving the excess. In a large nonstick skillet, heat the oil until hot but not smoking over medium-high heat. Add the chicken and cook until golden brown, 1 to 2 minutes per side.

2. Add the tomatoes, potatoes, mushrooms, prosciutto, broth, wine, garlic, and rosemary. Bring to a simmer, cover, and cook until the chicken is cooked through, about 10 minutes.

3. Meanwhile, in a jar with a tight-fitting lid, combine the reserved flour mixture and ¼ cup of water and shake until smooth. Stir the mixture and the remaining ¼ teaspoon salt into the pan and cook, stirring, until slightly thickened, about 3 minutes. Place the chicken on 4 plates, top with the sauce, and serve.

Helpful hint: Shaking the flour and water in a jar ensures a lump-free sauce. You can use this trick any time you make a starch-based gravy.

FAT: 5G/15%
CALORIES: 298
SATURATED FAT: .9G
CARBOHYDRATE: 29G
PROTEIN: 32G
CHOLESTEROL: 69MG
SODIUM: 513MG

The city of Bologna, in Emilia-Romagna, is surrounded by some of Italy's most fertile farmland. Garden vegetables abound, and farm animals thrive in the rich pastures. This typical chicken scallopini and vegetable dish takes advantage of the region's bounty. Asparagus—another prized product of the area—would be the perfect companion for the chicken.

Baked Stuffed Sole with Olives and Tomatoes

SERVES: 4
WORKING TIME: 20 MINUTES
TOTAL TIME: 40 MINUTES

In late summer, when locally grown beefsteak tomatoes are plentiful and cheap, try them in this unusual dish. The hefty tomato slices form the base for rolled fish fillets with a lemony olive stuffing. If you have a handsome ceramic baking dish, bring the sizzling fish straight from the oven to the table. Braised leeks make a delicate side dish for this assertively flavored entrée.

⅓ cup plus 1 tablespoon chopped fresh parsley

⅓ cup Calamata or other brine-cured olives, pitted and chopped

3 cloves garlic, minced

2 tablespoons plain dried bread crumbs

½ teaspoon grated lemon zest

2 tablespoons fresh lemon juice

¾ teaspoon dried oregano

4 sole or flounder fillets, any visible bones removed (about 1½ pounds total)

8 thick slices of tomato

¼ teaspoon salt

2 teaspoons olive oil

½ teaspoon paprika

1. Preheat the oven to 400°. In a small bowl, combine ⅓ cup of the parsley, the olives, garlic, bread crumbs, lemon zest, lemon juice, and oregano.

2. Lay the fillets flat, skinned-sides down. Spoon the parsley mixture over the fillets and, starting from a short side, roll up each fillet. Lay the tomato slices in a 9-inch square baking dish, slightly overlapping them. Sprinkle with the salt. Place the fillets, seam-sides down, on top of the tomatoes. Drizzle the fish rolls with the oil and sprinkle with the paprika. Cover with foil and bake for 20 minutes, or until the fish is just opaque in the center.

3. Divide the tomatoes among 4 plates. Top the tomatoes with the fish rolls, spoon the pan juices over the fish, sprinkle with the remaining 1 tablespoon parsley, and serve.

Helpful hint: Flounder has many names: Some types are identified as "sole" in supermarkets. Depending on where you live, you can buy various types of flounder called lemon sole, gray sole, rex sole, petrale, winter or summer flounder, starry flounder, witch flounder, fluke, or sand dab.

FAT: 8G/29%
CALORIES: 249
SATURATED FAT: 1.2G
CARBOHYDRATE: 10G
PROTEIN: 34G
CHOLESTEROL: 82MG
SODIUM: 513MG

For classic veal Milanese, veal scallopini are dipped in whole beaten eggs, coated with bread crumbs and Parmesan, and fried in butter. For this trimmed-down version, chicken breasts are dipped in Parmesan, egg whites, and bread crumbs, then baked in the oven with a mere drizzling of olive oil. Round out the meal with roasted new potatoes and Italian green beans.

CHICKEN MILANESE

SERVES: 4
WORKING TIME: 15 MINUTES
TOTAL TIME: 25 MINUTES

½ cup plain dried bread crumbs

¼ cup grated Parmesan cheese

1 egg white beaten with
1 tablespoon water

4 skinless, boneless chicken breast
halves (about 1 pound total)

2 teaspoons olive oil

⅔ cup dry white wine

½ cup reduced-sodium chicken
broth, defatted

2 tablespoons balsamic vinegar

3 cloves garlic, minced

2 teaspoons anchovy paste

½ teaspoon dried rosemary

1 teaspoon cornstarch mixed
with 1 tablespoon water

2 tablespoons chopped fresh
parsley

1. Preheat the oven to 400°. Line a large baking sheet with foil.

2. Place the bread crumbs, Parmesan, and egg white mixture in 3 shallow bowls. Dip the chicken into the Parmesan (see tip, top photo), then into the egg white (middle photo), and finally into the bread crumbs (bottom photo). Place the chicken on the prepared baking sheet and drizzle with the oil. Bake for 10 minutes, or until the chicken is cooked through and golden brown.

3. Meanwhile, in a large skillet, combine the wine, broth, vinegar, garlic, anchovy paste, and rosemary and bring to a boil over medium heat. Boil, stirring occasionally, until the garlic is tender and the sauce is slightly reduced, about 4 minutes. Stir in the cornstarch mixture and cook, stirring, until slightly thickened, about 1 minute. Add the parsley, stirring to combine. Add the chicken and turn to coat with the sauce. Place the chicken on 4 plates and serve.

Helpful hint: Anchovy paste comes in tubes, making it a convenient way to keep anchovies on hand. Keep the tube tightly capped and store it in the refrigerator. Anchovy paste will keep for 6 months or longer.

FAT: 6G/20%
CALORIES: 268
SATURATED FAT: 1.9G
CARBOHYDRATE: 12G
PROTEIN: 32G
CHOLESTEROL: 71MG
SODIUM: 491MG

CHICKEN RISOTTO

SERVES: 4
WORKING TIME: 25 MINUTES
TOTAL TIME: 50 MINUTES

Arborio rice—a "superfino" variety from Italy's Po Valley—is considered perfect for risotto. The grain's starchy exterior cooks to a creamy consistency, while the center remains slightly al dente. As traditionally prepared, risotto requires constant attention; the broth and wine are added very gradually, with constant stirring. You'll appreciate this more streamlined method.

2 teaspoons olive oil

¾ pound skinless, boneless chicken thighs, cut into 1-inch pieces

6 ounces mushrooms, thinly sliced

1 small onion, finely chopped

1½ cups Arborio rice

⅔ cup dry white wine

3 cups reduced-sodium chicken broth, defatted

¼ teaspoon salt

⅔ cup frozen peas, thawed

½ cup grated Parmesan cheese

2 teaspoons unsalted butter

½ teaspoon freshly ground black pepper

1. In a large nonstick saucepan, heat the oil until hot but not smoking over medium heat. Add the chicken and mushrooms and cook, stirring frequently, until the chicken is cooked through and the mushrooms are softened, about 3 minutes. With a slotted spoon, transfer the chicken and mushrooms to a bowl.

2. Stir the onion into the saucepan and cook, stirring occasionally, until the onion is softened, about 4 minutes. Add the rice, stir to coat, and add the wine. Cook until the wine has been absorbed, about 3 minutes. In a medium bowl, combine the broth and 1 cup of water. Add 2 cups of the broth mixture to the rice along with the salt, and cook, stirring occasionally, until the liquid has been absorbed, about 10 minutes.

3. Add 1 cup of the broth mixture to the pan and cook, stirring occasionally, until the liquid has been absorbed, about 5 minutes. Add the remaining 1 cup broth mixture and cook, stirring occasionally, until the risotto is creamy and the rice is tender but with a slight firmness at the center, about 5 minutes. Return the chicken and mushrooms to the pan and add the peas, Parmesan, butter, and pepper. Cook, stirring, until the Parmesan and butter are melted, about 2 minutes. Serve hot.

Helpful hint: You can use long-grain instead of Arborio rice if you like. It will cook in less time and the risotto will not be as creamy.

FAT: 11G/19%
CALORIES: 533
SATURATED FAT: 4.4G
CARBOHYDRATE: 69G
PROTEIN: 31G
CHOLESTEROL: 84MG
SODIUM: 911MG

BEEF BRACIOLE

SERVES: 4
WORKING TIME: 35 MINUTES
TOTAL TIME: 45 MINUTES

These tasty beef rolls (stuffed, rolled cutlets are called "braciole" in Italian) are made from lean round steak and are served over pasta.

1 cup frozen chopped spinach, thawed and squeezed dry

⅓ cup grated Parmesan cheese

¼ cup plain dried bread crumbs

2 tablespoons raisins

2 cloves garlic, minced

1 pound well-trimmed top round of beef, cut into 8 slices

2 tablespoons flour

¾ teaspoon salt

¾ teaspoon freshly ground black pepper

2 teaspoons olive oil

½ cup dry red wine

2 cups chopped plum tomatoes

½ teaspoon dried oregano

½ teaspoon cornstarch mixed with 1 teaspoon water

¼ cup chopped fresh parsley

8 ounces rigatoni pasta

1. In a small bowl, combine the spinach, 3 tablespoons of the Parmesan, the bread crumbs, raisins, and garlic. With a meat pounder, pound the beef to a ¼-inch thickness. Dividing evenly, spread the spinach mixture on the beef, and roll up from one short end. Secure with a toothpick.

2. On a sheet of waxed paper, combine the flour, ¼ teaspoon of the salt, and ¼ teaspoon of the pepper. Dredge the beef rolls in the flour mixture, shaking off the excess. In a large nonstick skillet, heat the oil until hot but not smoking over medium-high heat. Add the beef rolls, seam-sides down, and cook until browned, about 4 minutes.

3. Add the wine to the skillet and boil for 1 minute. Reduce the heat to medium, add the tomatoes, oregano, and the remaining ½ teaspoon each salt and pepper. Bring to a boil, reduce to a simmer, cover, and cook until the beef is tender, about 12 minutes. Transfer the beef to a cutting board, remove the toothpicks, and cut the rolls into ½-inch slices. Stir the cornstarch mixture and parsley into the skillet and cook, stirring, until slightly thickened, about 1 minute.

4. Meanwhile, in a large pot of boiling water, cook the pasta until tender. Drain well. Place the pasta on 4 plates, top with the sauce and braciole, sprinkle the remaining Parmesan on top, and serve.

FAT: 10G/17%
CALORIES: 518
SATURATED FAT: 3.1G
CARBOHYDRATE: 62G
PROTEIN: 40G
CHOLESTEROL: 70MG
SODIUM: 708MG

SIDE DISHES

4

HERBED STUFFED ZUCCHINI WITH PROSCIUTTO

SERVES: 4
WORKING TIME: 25 MINUTES
TOTAL TIME: 40 MINUTES

Italian cooks have a repertoire of fillings for a wide variety of vegetables; some are side dishes, some hearty main courses. For this light "zucchini ripiene" (stuffed zucchini), the squash flesh is scooped out, seasoned with prosciutto, onions, garlic, and herbs, and returned to the shells to bake. Try it with savory broiled swordfish.

Four 6-ounce zucchini, halved lengthwise

½ cup reduced-sodium chicken broth, defatted

1 onion, finely chopped

2 cloves garlic, minced

3 tablespoons (1 ounce) finely chopped prosciutto or Canadian bacon

3 tablespoons grated Parmesan cheese

2 tablespoons no-salt-added tomato paste

½ teaspoon dried rosemary

½ teaspoon dried oregano

¼ teaspoon salt

2 tablespoons plain dried bread crumbs

1. Preheat the oven to 400°. With a small spoon, scoop out the flesh of the zucchini, leaving a ¼-inch border all around. Coarsely chop the flesh and reserve.

2. In a small nonstick skillet, combine the broth, onion, garlic, and prosciutto. Cook over medium heat, stirring frequently, until the onion is softened, about 5 minutes. Add the reserved zucchini flesh and cook, stirring frequently, until the zucchini is barely tender, about 4 minutes. Transfer the onion mixture to a medium bowl. Stir in 2 tablespoons of the Parmesan, the tomato paste, rosemary, oregano, and salt.

3. Place the zucchini on a baking sheet and spoon in the onion filling. In a small bowl, combine the remaining 1 tablespoon Parmesan and the bread crumbs and sprinkle over the stuffed zucchini. Bake for 15 minutes, until the zucchini is tender and the filling is piping hot.

Helpful hint: To add color to the meal, use two green zucchini and two golden ones, serving each person a green half and a golden half.

FAT: 3G/26%
CALORIES: 104
SATURATED FAT: 1.1G
CARBOHYDRATE: 15G
PROTEIN: 7G
CHOLESTEROL: 9MG
SODIUM: 458MG

ITALIAN GREEN BEANS WITH GARLIC AND TOMATOES

SERVES: 4
WORKING TIME: 20 MINUTES
TOTAL TIME: 30 MINUTES

1 teaspoon olive oil

1 onion, finely chopped

3 cloves garlic, slivered

1½ cups chopped tomatoes

½ cup chopped fresh basil

½ teaspoon salt

1 teaspoon hot pepper sauce

Two 10-ounce packages frozen Italian flat green beans

1. In a large nonstick skillet, heat the oil until hot but not smoking over medium heat. Add the onion and garlic and cook, stirring frequently, until the onion is softened, about 7 minutes.

2. Add the tomatoes, basil, salt, and hot pepper sauce and bring to a boil. Add the beans, reduce the heat to a simmer, and cook until the beans are tender, about 8 minutes.

Helpful hint: If you can get fresh Italian flat green beans, use them in place of the frozen. The cooking times will be approximately the same, depending on the size of the fresh beans. Test them after 8 minutes and if they are still too raw, continue cooking them, with the skillet covered.

FAT: 2G/19%
CALORIES: 96
SATURATED FAT: .3G
CARBOHYDRATE: 20G
PROTEIN: 4G
CHOLESTEROL: 0MG
SODIUM: 319MG

This colorful vegetable toss will brighten a meal centered on simple chicken breasts or pork cutlets. The flavors are as bright as the jade-green beans and crimson tomatoes: There's garlic, fresh basil, and peppery heat. Add the hot sauce in small increments to taste—half the amount called for here may be enough for some.

*I*talians love artichokes, which in Italy appear in the market in a variety of shapes and sizes. A high-fat sauce often accompanies these velvet-fleshed vegetables, but this luxurious dip is based on reduced-fat mayonnaise and mashed garlic. Stuffed swordfish and rosemary-flavored potatoes would make a lovely meal with the artichokes.

ARTICHOKES WITH GARLIC "MAYONNAISE"

SERVES: 4
WORKING TIME: 20 MINUTES
TOTAL TIME: 45 MINUTES

1 all-purpose potato (6 ounces), peeled and thinly sliced

4 cloves garlic, peeled

¼ cup fresh lemon juice

3 tablespoons reduced-fat mayonnaise

3 tablespoons reduced-sodium chicken broth, defatted

¾ teaspoon dried rosemary

¾ teaspoon dried marjoram

½ teaspoon salt

4 large artichokes (12 ounces each)

3 tablespoons chopped fresh parsley

1. In a small pot of boiling water, cook the potato until tender, about 12 minutes. Add the garlic during the last 3 minutes of cooking. Drain. Transfer to a large bowl and mash until smooth. Add 2 tablespoons of the lemon juice, the mayonnaise, broth, ¼ teaspoon of the rosemary, ¼ teaspoon of the marjoram, and the salt. Set aside.

2. In a large pot, combine 3½ cups of water, the remaining 2 table-spoons lemon juice, the remaining ½ teaspoon rosemary, and remaining ½ teaspoon marjoram. Bring to a boil over high heat.

3. Meanwhile, pull off the tough bottom leaves of the artichoke (see tip; top photo). With kitchen shears, snip the sharp, pointed ends from the remaining leaves (middle photo). With a paring knife, trim off the end of the stem (bottom photo). Add the artichokes to the boiling liquid, cover, and cook until the artichokes are tender, about 25 minutes. Stir the parsley into the garlic "mayonnaise" and serve with the artichokes.

Helpful hint: To eat an artichoke, pull off the outer leaves one at a time and scrape the fleshy base from each leaf by drawing it between your front teeth. When you've finished the leaves, remove the prickly "choke" from the artichoke bottom before eating it.

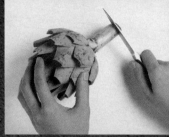

FAT: 3G/21%
CALORIES: 130
SATURATED FAT: .4G
CARBOHYDRATE: 25G
PROTEIN: 6G
CHOLESTEROL: 0MG
SODIUM: 525MG

Roasted Potatoes with Parmesan and Herbs

Serves: 4
Working time: 15 minutes
Total time: 45 minutes

When you cook potatoes in the pan along with a roast or bird, the result is undeniably delicious but unfortunately loaded with fat. The potatoes absorb the fat that runs off from the meat. But even with a spoonful of olive oil and a generous sprinkling of Parmesan, these "al forno" (oven-cooked) potatoes are a healthier choice. Try them with sage-rubbed roasted game hens.

1½ pounds small red potatoes
1 tablespoon extra-virgin olive oil
3 cloves garlic, peeled and halved
¾ teaspoon dried rosemary
½ teaspoon dried sage
1½ teaspoons grated lemon zest
½ teaspoon salt
¼ cup grated Parmesan cheese

1. Preheat the oven to 400°. With a vegetable peeler, peel a thin band around the circumference of each potato. In a large pot of boiling water, cook the potatoes for 5 minutes. Drain.

2. In a large roasting pan, combine the oil, garlic, rosemary, and sage. Bake until the garlic is fragrant and the oil is hot, about 4 minutes. Add the potatoes, lemon zest, and salt and bake, turning occasionally, for 20 minutes, or until the potatoes are crisp, golden, and tender. Sprinkle the Parmesan over the potatoes and bake for 2 minutes, or just until the cheese is melted and golden brown.

Helpful hint: If you're in a hurry, you can skip the peeling step and roast the potatoes with their skins on.

Fat: 5g/23%
Calories: 193
Saturated Fat: 1.4g
Carbohydrate: 32g
Protein: 6g
Cholesterol: 4mg
Sodium: 380mg

Baked Mushrooms with Parmesan and Basil

SERVES: 4
WORKING TIME: 20 MINUTES
TOTAL TIME: 30 MINUTES

Beefy portobellos topped with slivers of melted Parmesan make a tasty, hearty side dish for any meal.

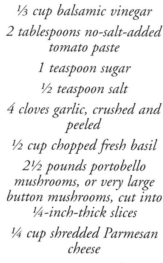

⅓ cup balsamic vinegar

2 tablespoons no-salt-added tomato paste

1 teaspoon sugar

½ teaspoon salt

4 cloves garlic, crushed and peeled

½ cup chopped fresh basil

2½ pounds portobello mushrooms, or very large button mushrooms, cut into ¼-inch-thick slices

¼ cup shredded Parmesan cheese

1 teaspoon cornstarch mixed with 1 tablespoon water

1. In a large shallow baking dish, combine the vinegar, tomato paste, sugar, and salt. Add the garlic and 2 tablespoons of the basil, stirring to combine. Add the mushrooms, tossing to coat. Set aside.

2. Preheat the oven to 400°. With a slotted spoon, transfer the mushrooms and garlic to a 13-x-9-inch baking pan; reserve the marinade. Bake the mushrooms for 8 minutes, or until tender. Remove and discard the garlic. Sprinkle the cheese over the mushrooms and bake for 2 minutes, or just until the cheese has begun to melt.

3. Meanwhile, strain the reserved marinade into a small saucepan and bring to a boil over medium heat. Stir in the cornstarch mixture and cook, stirring, until slightly thickened, about 1 minute. Stir in the remaining 6 tablespoons basil. Spoon the sauce onto 4 plates and top with the mushrooms.

Helpful hint: Combining the cornstarch with cold water before adding it to the boiling marinade helps keep the cornstarch from lumping. To further ensure a lump-free sauce, stir or whisk the marinade constantly as you add the cornstarch mixture.

FAT: 2G/24%
CALORIES: 75
SATURATED FAT: 1G
CARBOHYDRATE: 11G
PROTEIN: 5G
CHOLESTEROL: 4MG
SODIUM: 375MG

POLENTA WITH TOMATO-MUSHROOM SAUCE

SERVES: 4
WORKING TIME: 20 MINUTES
TOTAL TIME: 40 MINUTES

1 teaspoon olive oil

3 cloves garlic, minced

½ pound mushrooms, thinly sliced

⅔ cup reduced-sodium chicken broth, defatted

8-ounce can no-salt-added tomato sauce

¾ teaspoon salt

¼ teaspoon dried rosemary

¼ teaspoon ground ginger

⅛ teaspoon red pepper flakes

1 cup yellow cornmeal

½ cup crumbled Gorgonzola cheese (2 ounces)

1. In a large nonstick skillet, heat the oil until hot but not smoking over medium heat. Add the garlic and cook until fragrant, about 1 minute. Add the mushrooms and broth and bring to a boil. Reduce to a simmer, cover, and cook until the mushrooms are softened, about 3 minutes. Add the tomato sauce, ¼ teaspoon of the salt, the rosemary, ginger, and red pepper flakes. Cook until the sauce is slightly reduced and the flavors are blended, about 5 minutes. Set aside.

2. In a medium bowl, combine the cornmeal and 1 cup of water. In a medium saucepan, bring 1½ cups of water to a boil over medium heat. Add the remaining ½ teaspoon of salt and reduce to a gentle simmer. Stirring constantly, gradually add the cornmeal mixture. Cook until the mixture is thick and leaves the sides of the pan, about 7 minutes. Add the Gorgonzola and stir until melted.

3. Gently reheat the tomato-mushroom sauce over low heat. Serve the polenta topped with the sauce.

Helpful hints: Although polenta is often cooked and then cooled in a pan, making it stiff enough to slice, this method yields a soft, creamy dish, about as thick as mashed potatoes. If you don't care for blue cheese, you can use shredded Fontina or Monterey jack.

FAT: 7G/28%
CALORIES: 227
SATURATED FAT: 3.2G
CARBOHYDRATE: 35G
PROTEIN: 9G
CHOLESTEROL: 13MG
SODIUM: 731MG

This tasty polenta can take the starring role alongside a simple main dish, such as baked haddock or cod.

SICILIAN ORANGE SALAD

SERVES: 4
WORKING TIME: 20 MINUTES
TOTAL TIME: 20 MINUTES

Although this traditional Italian salad is sometimes served between courses to freshen the palate, it would also be welcome alongside a rich and savory entrée such as a stuffed beef roast. We've added the peppery bite of watercress for an even more refreshing dish; arugula would be a tasty alternative. Plump green Sicilian olives lend an authentic touch.

6 navel oranges
3 tablespoons honey
2 tablespoons red wine vinegar
1 tablespoon extra-virgin olive oil
2 teaspoons Dijon mustard
½ teaspoon salt
⅛ teaspoon red pepper flakes
2 bunches watercress, tough stems removed
1 red onion, halved and thinly sliced
¼ cup slivered green olives

1. With a small knife, remove the peel and trim away all the bitter white pith from the oranges. Working over a sieve set over a large bowl to catch the juices, cut between the membranes to release the orange segments. Squeeze the membranes to get a total of ½ cup of juice. Set the segments aside.

2. Add the honey, vinegar, oil, mustard, salt, and red pepper flakes to the orange juice, whisking to blend. Add the watercress, onion, orange segments, and olives, tossing well to combine.

Helpful hint: If you can't find Sicilian olives, you can use purple-black Greek Calamatas instead.

FAT: 5G/21%
CALORIES: 215
SATURATED FAT: .7G
CARBOHYDRATE: 43G
PROTEIN: 5G
CHOLESTEROL: 0MG
SODIUM: 580MG

TOMATOES WITH HERBED CROUTON STUFFING

SERVES: 4
WORKING TIME: 20 MINUTES
TOTAL TIME: 40 MINUTES

4 ounces Italian bread, cut into ½-inch slices

2 cloves garlic, peeled and halved

¼ cup chopped fresh basil

¼ cup reduced-sodium chicken broth, defatted

2 tablespoons capers

2 teaspoons olive oil

¼ teaspoon salt

¼ teaspoon freshly ground black pepper

¼ teaspoon nutmeg

4 large tomatoes (8 ounces each)

1. Preheat the oven to 400°. Rub the bread with the cut sides of the garlic and then cut the bread into small cubes. Bake, turning once, for 6 minutes, or until lightly toasted. Transfer the bread cubes to a large bowl. Add the basil, 2 tablespoons of the broth, the capers, oil, salt, pepper, and nutmeg.

2. With a serrated knife, cut a ½-inch slice from the stem end of each tomato. With a small spoon, scoop the seeds and a little of the pulp out of the tomatoes (leaving a ½-inch-thick wall inside each tomato) and discard. Place the tomato shells in a shallow baking dish, spoon the bread mixture into the tomatoes, sprinkle with the remaining 2 tablespoons broth, and bake for 15 minutes, or until piping hot.

Helpful hint: If you have a little extra time, place the seeded tomatoes upside down on paper towels and let stand for 15 minutes or so to drain off any excess liquid.

Arrange these plump stuffed tomatoes on a platter with grilled steaks, chops, or chicken breasts for an instantly festive meal. The garlicky croutons that fill the tomatoes are oven-toasted, not fried like traditional croutons.

FAT: 4G/26%
CALORIES: 140
SATURATED FAT: .7G
CARBOHYDRATE: 24G
PROTEIN: 4G
CHOLESTEROL: 0MG
SODIUM: 467MG

*T*hese little stuffed pepper "cups" are knife-and-fork fare at the table, but they're also ideal for a buffet, where they could serve as finger food. At a sit-down meal, partner the peppers with a pork roast or chops; at a buffet, include them with a selection of other vegetable side dishes.

SICILIAN-STYLE STUFFED PEPPER WEDGES

SERVES: 4
WORKING TIME: 15 MINUTES
TOTAL TIME: 45 MINUTES

4 bell peppers, mixed colors

1 tomato, coarsely chopped

⅓ cup plain dried bread crumbs

¼ cup raisins, coarsely chopped

1 tablespoon capers, rinsed and drained

1 tablespoon anchovy paste

2 teaspoons extra-virgin olive oil

½ teaspoon dried oregano

¼ teaspoon salt

¼ teaspoon freshly ground black pepper

1. Preheat the oven to 425°. Spray a large baking sheet with nonstick cooking spray.

2. Cut the tops off the bell peppers and quarter the peppers lengthwise (see tip). Stem the reserved pepper tops and coarsely chop the flesh. Set aside.

3. In a medium bowl, combine the chopped pepper tops, tomato, bread crumbs, raisins, capers, anchovy paste, oil, oregano, salt, and black pepper. Place the pepper quarters, cut-sides up, on the prepared baking sheet. Spoon the tomato mixture into the peppers and bake for 20 minutes, or until the filling is piping hot and the peppers are softened.

Helpful hint: It will be easier to chop the raisins if you first chill them in the freezer for 20 to 30 minutes, and spray the knife blade with nonstick cooking spray, too.

FAT: 4G/29%
CALORIES: 121
SATURATED FAT: .6G
CARBOHYDRATE: 20G
PROTEIN: 4G
CHOLESTEROL: 3MG
SODIUM: 437MG

TIP

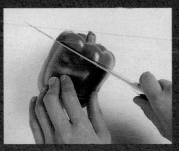

Cut off about ½ inch from the tops of the bell peppers and reserve. Halve the peppers lengthwise and remove the seeds and membranes. Halve each pepper half again to make 4 quarters.

CAULIFLOWER MILANESE

SERVES: 4
WORKING TIME: 15 MINUTES
TOTAL TIME: 40 MINUTES

The bread crumbs and Parmesan that top the cauliflower are what make this "Milanese." However, we've omitted one traditional Milanese ingredient— butter—and substituted a touch of olive oil for a more healthful dish. A deep-toned bowl, like the green one used here, displays the pale golden vegetable to good advantage.

5 cups cauliflower florets

½ cup reduced-sodium chicken broth, defatted

¾ teaspoon grated lemon zest

½ teaspoon salt

½ teaspoon dried marjoram

¼ teaspoon freshly ground black pepper

¼ cup plain dried bread crumbs

2 tablespoons grated Parmesan cheese

1 teaspoon olive oil

2 teaspoons fresh lemon juice

1. Preheat the oven to 400°. In a large pot of boiling water, cook the cauliflower for 4 minutes to blanch. Drain well.

2. Meanwhile, in a small bowl, combine the broth, lemon zest, salt, marjoram, and pepper. Set aside. In another small bowl, combine the bread crumbs and Parmesan. Set aside.

3. Spread the oil in a 13-x-9-inch baking dish and heat in the oven until hot, about 4 minutes. Add the cauliflower to the baking dish and bake, stirring occasionally, for 7 minutes, or until the cauliflower is golden. Pour the reserved broth mixture over the cauliflower and bake for 7 minutes, or until the cauliflower is tender. Sprinkle the bread crumb mixture over the cauliflower, drizzle with the lemon juice, and bake for 5 minutes, or until the topping is lightly crisped.

Helpful hint: When shopping for cauliflower, choose a firm head that's creamy white with crisp, green leaves at the base. Pass up heads that have dark speckles or soft spots.

FAT: 3G/22%
CALORIES: 82
SATURATED FAT: .7G
CARBOHYDRATE: 12G
PROTEIN: 5G
CHOLESTEROL: 2MG
SODIUM: 478MG

Risi e Bisi

Serves: 4
Working time: 25 minutes
Total time: 25 minutes

Italians celebrate spring—and the accompanying advent of the first green peas—with a bowl of this soothing, delicately flavored dish of rice and peas. The frozen small peas sometimes labeled "petit pois" are best for this recipe. You could also use tiny fresh peas; add them to the pan along with the onion.

2 teaspoons olive oil

2 tablespoons chopped pancetta or Canadian bacon

1 small onion, finely chopped

1 cup long-grain rice

2 cups reduced-sodium chicken broth, defatted

2 tablespoons dry white wine

2 cups frozen peas, thawed

3 tablespoons chopped fresh parsley

3 tablespoons grated Parmesan cheese

½ teaspoon salt

⅛ teaspoon freshly ground black pepper

1. In a large nonstick skillet, heat the oil until hot but not smoking over medium heat. Add the pancetta and onion and cook until the onion is softened, about 5 minutes.

2. Stir the rice into the skillet and cook, stirring occasionally, until lightly golden, about 3 minutes. Add the broth and wine and bring to a boil. Reduce to a simmer, cover, and cook for 15 minutes. Remove from the heat and stir in the peas, parsley, Parmesan, salt, and pepper. Let stand, covered, for 5 minutes before serving.

Helpful hint: If you are substituting fresh peas for frozen, you'll need 2 pounds of peas in the pod, which will yield 2 cups. Depending on the size of the peas, you may have to cook them a few minutes extra in step 1.

Fat: 4g/12%
Calories: 294
Saturated Fat: 1.2g
Carbohydrate: 50g
Protein: 12g
Cholesterol: 5mg
Sodium: 814mg

Baked Eggplant with Herbs and Lemon

Serves: 4
Working time: 20 minutes
Total time: 45 minutes

Baking (rather than frying) eggplant minimizes the fat content of this dish: A Parmesan crust and a zesty tomato sauce ensure full flavor.

⅔ cup plain dried bread crumbs

3 tablespoons grated Parmesan cheese

1¼ teaspoons grated lemon zest

¾ teaspoon dried oregano

¾ teaspoon dried thyme

3 egg whites

1 eggplant (1 pound), peeled and sliced into 16 rounds

2 teaspoons olive oil

2 teaspoons fresh lemon juice

8-ounce can no-salt-added tomato sauce

¼ teaspoon salt

1. Preheat the oven to 400°. Line a baking sheet with foil.

2. On a plate, combine the bread crumbs, Parmesan cheese, ¾ teaspoon of the lemon zest, ¼ teaspoon of the oregano, and ¼ teaspoon of the thyme. In a shallow bowl, beat the egg whites with 2 tablespoons of water. Dip each eggplant round into the egg whites, then into the bread crumb mixture, and place on the prepared baking sheet.

3. In a small bowl, combine the oil and lemon juice and drizzle the mixture over the eggplant slices. Bake for 25 minutes, or until crisp and golden brown. Transfer the eggplant to a serving platter.

4. Meanwhile, in a small saucepan, combine the tomato sauce, salt, the remaining ½ teaspoon lemon zest, remaining ½ teaspoon oregano, and remaining ½ teaspoon thyme. Bring to a boil over medium heat. Reduce to a simmer and cook for 2 minutes to blend the flavors. Spoon the sauce over the eggplant and serve.

Helpful hint: Although eggplant looks like a sturdy vegetable, it's actually thin-skinned and quite perishable. Use eggplant within 5 days of purchase; as it ages, the vegetable may turn bitter.

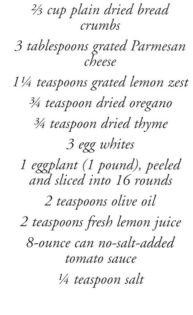

Fat: 5g/27%
Calories: 168
Saturated Fat: 1.2g
Carbohydrate: 24g
Protein: 8g
Cholesterol: 3mg
Sodium: 418mg

CANNELLINI WITH SAGE AND ROMANO CHEESE

SERVES: 4
WORKING TIME: 25 MINUTES
TOTAL TIME: 25 MINUTES

1 tablespoon extra-virgin olive oil

1 large onion, finely chopped

3 cloves garlic, minced

1 rib celery, halved lengthwise and thinly sliced

1 tomato, finely chopped

½ cup reduced-sodium chicken broth, defatted

1 tablespoon chopped fresh sage, or ½ teaspoon dried sage

½ teaspoon freshly ground black pepper

¼ teaspoon salt

Two 19-ounce cans white kidney beans (cannellini), rinsed and drained

2 tablespoons grated Romano cheese

1. In a large nonstick saucepan, heat 1 teaspoon of the oil until hot but not smoking over medium heat. Add the onion and garlic and cook, stirring frequently, until the onion is softened, about 5 minutes. Stir in the celery and cook until the celery is softened, about 4 minutes.

2. Stir in the tomato, broth, sage, pepper, and salt and bring to a boil. Add the beans, reduce to a simmer, cover, and cook until the flavors are blended and the beans are rich and creamy, about 5 minutes. Stir in the Romano and the remaining 2 teaspoons oil and serve.

Helpful hint: If you prefer a milder flavor, substitute Parmesan cheese for the sharper Romano.

FAT: 6G/20%
CALORIES: 266
SATURATED FAT: .6G
CARBOHYDRATE: 38G
PROTEIN: 16G
CHOLESTEROL: 3MG
SODIUM: 594MG

Serve Tuscany's signature bean dish with grilled game hens, an arugula salad, and a Tuscan Trebbiano wine.

Pepper, Zucchini, and Potato Tiella

SERVES: 4
WORKING TIME: 15 MINUTES
TOTAL TIME: 35 MINUTES

1 pound small red potatoes, halved

1 tablespoon olive oil

2 cloves garlic, peeled and halved

¾ teaspoon dried oregano

½ teaspoon dried rosemary

½ teaspoon dried sage

1 red onion, cut into 1-inch chunks

1 red bell pepper, cut into ½-inch-wide strips

2 zucchini, halved lengthwise and cut into 1-inch pieces

1 tomato, coarsely chopped

½ teaspoon salt

1. Preheat the oven to 400°. In a large pot of boiling water, cook the potatoes for 5 minutes to blanch. Drain well.

2. In a 13-x-9-inch baking dish, combine the oil, garlic, oregano, rosemary, and sage. Bake until the oil is hot and the herbs are fragrant, about 5 minutes. Add the potatoes, onion, bell pepper, zucchini, tomato, and salt, stirring to combine. Bake, stirring occasionally, for 25 minutes, or until the vegetables are tender. Divide among 4 plates and serve hot or at room temperature.

Helpful hint: Any kind of summer squash can go into this casserole. Golden zucchini, patty pan (white or yellow), yellow crookneck, or yellow straightneck would all work well.

The province of Apulia, which forms the "heel" of the boot-shaped Italian peninsula, is home to the layered casserole called "tiella." The dish is infinitely variable, but is almost always made with potatoes. Peppers, onions, and tomatoes are other common ingredients. In this casual tiella, the vegetables are stirred together rather than layered.

FAT: 4G/22%
CALORIES: 166
SATURATED FAT: .5G
CARBOHYDRATE: 30G
PROTEIN: 4G
CHOLESTEROL: 0MG
SODIUM: 293MG

Winter
squash, surprisingly, is
a familiar ingredient
in Italian cooking—
especially in the cool
northern province of
Lombardy, where it is
grown. In this
substantial side dish,
the tang of red wine
vinegar balances the
sweetness of the sugar
and raisins; chopped
mint adds a refreshing
note. Serve the squash
with chicken or fish
rolls, or with a light
pasta dish.

BUTTERNUT SQUASH WITH MINT AND ALMONDS

SERVES: 4
WORKING TIME: 15 MINUTES
TOTAL TIME: 35 MINUTES

2 teaspoons olive oil

1 large red onion, cut into ½-inch chunks

2 cloves garlic, minced

1 butternut squash (1¾ pounds), peeled, seeded, and cut into ¾-inch chunks (see tip)

1 tablespoon sugar

3 tablespoons red wine vinegar

½ cup reduced-sodium chicken broth, defatted

½ teaspoon salt

¼ cup chopped fresh mint

2 tablespoons golden raisins

1 tablespoon sliced almonds

1. In a large nonstick skillet, heat the oil until hot but not smoking over medium heat. Add the onion and garlic and cook, stirring frequently, until the onion is softened, about 5 minutes.

2. Add the squash, tossing to coat. Sprinkle with the sugar and cook for 1 minute or until the sugar is melted. Add the vinegar and cook just until the vinegar has evaporated, about 2 minutes. Stir in the broth and salt and bring to a boil. Reduce to a simmer, cover, and cook until the squash is tender, about 10 minutes. Add the mint and raisins and cook, uncovered, until slightly reduced, about 3 minutes. Sprinkle the almonds on top and serve.

Helpful hint: You can substitute smaller winter squash, such as acorn or sweet dumpling, though butternut will be the easiest to peel because of its smoothly rounded shape and relatively thin skin.

FAT: 3G/17%
CALORIES: 159
SATURATED FAT: .4G
CARBOHYDRATE: 33G
PROTEIN: 4G
CHOLESTEROL: 0MG
SODIUM: 368MG

TIP

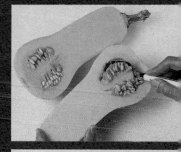

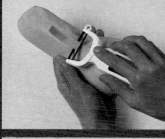

To prepare butternut squash, halve it lengthwise, scoop out the seeds, and peel. Cut the squash halves lengthwise into ¾-inch wide pieces, then cut crosswise into uniform ¾-inch cubes.

ONIONS AGRODOLCE

SERVES: 4
WORKING TIME: 15 MINUTES
TOTAL TIME: 20 MINUTES

Here's a unique and easy accompaniment for roast pork or poultry. The classic recipe for onions in "agrodolce" (sweet-and-sour sauce) is not quite so quick and easy: Small whole onions need to be braised for as long as two hours to become completely tender. The frozen pearl onions we've used cook in about ten minutes— and of course you don't have to peel them, either.

1 teaspoon olive oil

1 pound frozen pearl onions, thawed

2 tablespoons sugar

½ teaspoon salt

½ cup reduced-sodium chicken broth, defatted

⅓ cup red wine vinegar

1 teaspoon unsalted butter

2 tablespoons chopped fresh parsley

2 tablespoons chopped fresh mint

1. In a large nonstick skillet, heat the oil until hot but not smoking over medium heat. Add the pearl onions and cook, shaking the pan, until the onions are nicely coated, about 2 minutes. Sprinkle the sugar and salt over the onions and continue cooking and shaking the pan until the sugar is melted and bubbly, about 3 minutes.

2. Add the broth and vinegar, reduce the heat to a simmer, and cook until the sauce is slightly syrupy and the onions are tender, about 4 minutes. Remove from the heat, stir in the butter, parsley, and mint and serve.

Helpful hint: You can serve the onions chilled if you like; but if you do so, leave out the butter, which will solidify when cool and give the dish an unappealing texture.

FAT: 2G/20%
CALORIES: 89
SATURATED FAT: .7G
CARBOHYDRATE: 17G
PROTEIN: 2G
CHOLESTEROL: 3MG
SODIUM: 366MG

Sautéed Spinach with Sun-Dried Tomatoes

SERVES: 4
WORKING TIME: 10 MINUTES
TOTAL TIME: 20 MINUTES

ake a lovely meatless meal of a big baked potato and this garlicky spinach; it's sautéed with bits of sweet sun-dried tomatoes.

½ cup sun-dried (not oil-packed) tomato halves
1 cup boiling water
2 teaspoons olive oil
2 cloves garlic, minced
⅛ teaspoon red pepper flakes
2 pounds fresh spinach leaves
½ teaspoon salt
⅛ teaspoon sugar
¼ cup reduced-sodium chicken broth, defatted

1. In a small bowl, combine the sun-dried tomatoes and boiling water and let stand until the tomatoes have softened, about 15 minutes. Drain the tomatoes, reserving ¼ cup of the soaking liquid. Coarsely chop the tomatoes and set aside.

2. In a large nonstick skillet, heat the oil until hot but not smoking over medium heat. Add the garlic, red pepper flakes, spinach, salt, sugar, and broth and cook just until the garlic is fragrant, about 3 minutes. Add the sun-dried tomatoes and the reserved soaking liquid. Cover and cook just until the spinach is wilted, about 4 minutes. Spoon onto 4 plates and serve.

Helpful hint: Sand and grit will rinse out of spinach more quickly if you rinse the leaves in lukewarm, rather than ice-cold, tap water.

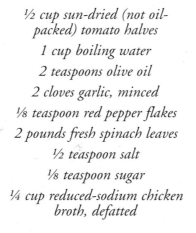

FAT: 3G/28%
CALORIES: 98
SATURATED FAT: .4G
CARBOHYDRATE: 14G
PROTEIN: 8G
CHOLESTEROL: 0MG
SODIUM: 501MG

DESSERTS

5

LATTE COTTA

You won't find a recipe for this velvety chocolate pudding in a standard Italian cookbook; it's our lightened version of a classic called "panne cotta" (cooked cream), made with "latte" (milk) instead. We don't stop with the cream though—we cut more fat by using cocoa powder rather than chocolate. Crumbled amaretti cookies make a crunchy topping.

1 envelope unflavored gelatin
2¼ cups low-fat (1%) milk
¼ cup unsweetened cocoa powder
¾ teaspoon cinnamon
¼ cup boiling water
½ cup firmly packed dark brown sugar
⅛ teaspoon salt
¾ teaspoon vanilla extract
6 amaretti cookies, crumbled

1. In a small bowl, sprinkle the gelatin over ¼ cup of the milk and let stand until softened, about 3 minutes. In another small bowl, combine the cocoa powder and cinnamon. Gradually add the boiling water to the cocoa mixture, whisking until smooth and no lumps remain. Set aside.

2. In a medium saucepan, combine the remaining 2 cups milk, the brown sugar, and salt. Whisk in the cocoa mixture until well combined. Bring to a boil over medium heat. Reduce the heat to a simmer, whisk in the gelatin mixture, and remove from the heat. Stir in the vanilla.

3. Divide the mixture among four 6-ounce dessert dishes and chill until set, about 2 hours. Sprinkle the amaretti cookies on top and serve.

Helpful hint: For a lump-free pudding, you will need lump-free brown sugar. If your sugar has hardened into rock-like pellets, place it in a microwavable dish and sprinkle it lightly with water; cover and cook on high power for 30 seconds.

FAT: 2G/12%
CALORIES: 145
SATURATED FAT: .9G
CARBOHYDRATE: 29G
PROTEIN: 5G
CHOLESTEROL: 4MG
SODIUM: 105MG

When Italians dine at home they are more likely to close a meal with fruit and cheese than with cake and pastries. This sophisticated finale draws on the time-honored combination of pears and blue cheese; here, it's Italy's fine Gorgonzola that fills the spiced pears. If you're not a fan of blue cheese, try this recipe using a mild goat cheese, such as Montrachet.

POACHED PEARS STUFFED WITH GORGONZOLA

SERVES: 4
WORKING TIME: 20 MINUTES
TOTAL TIME: 30 MINUTES

1½ cups dry white wine

⅓ cup sugar

1 cinnamon stick

¼ teaspoon allspice berries

¼ teaspoon whole black peppercorns

4 firm-ripe pears, such as Bosc or Bartlett, peeled, halved, and cored

¾ cup crumbled Gorgonzola or goat cheese (3 ounces)

1 tablespoon reduced-fat cream cheese (Neufchâtel)

1. In a large saucepan big enough to fit 8 pear halves in a single layer, combine the wine, sugar, cinnamon, allspice, and peppercorns. Bring to a boil over medium heat, add the pears, and reduce the heat to a simmer. Place a piece of waxed paper directly over the pears (to keep them from becoming discolored) and simmer gently until the pears are just tender when pierced with a fork, about 7 minutes. Remove the waxed paper and with a slotted spoon, transfer the pears to a plate.

2. Bring the wine mixture to a boil over high heat. Cook until the liquid is reduced to a syrup thick enough to coat the back of a spoon, about 5 minutes. Strain through a fine-mesh sieve and cool to room temperature.

3. In a small bowl, mash the Gorgonzola and cream cheeses until well blended. Spoon the cheese mixture into a pastry bag with no tip attached (or use a sturdy plastic bag; see tip). Pipe the cheese mixture into the hollow of the pears. Divide the pears among 4 plates, spoon the reduced wine syrup over, and serve.

Helpful Hint: Ground spices will make the poaching liquid murky in appearance, but if you don't have allspice berries, peppercorns, or cinnamon sticks on hand, you can use ⅛ teaspoon ground allspice, ¼ teaspoon ground cinnamon, and ¼ teaspoon freshly ground black pepper.

FAT: 8G/26%
CALORIES: 279
SATURATED FAT: 5G
CARBOHYDRATE: 43G
PROTEIN: 6G
CHOLESTEROL: 21MG
SODIUM: 316MG

TIP

If you don't own a pastry bag, spoon the cheese mixture into a large, sturdy plastic bag. Twist the top of the bag closed, and snip off one bottom corner with scissors. Squeezing the bag gently, pipe the filling evenly into the pear halves.

Caramelized Oranges with Toasted Almonds

Serves: 4
Working time: 10 minutes
Total time: 15 minutes

Bring a touch of sun-washed southern Italy to your table with these glowing, sweetly glazed orange slices. Be sure to buy eating oranges (rather than juice oranges) for this recipe. Navel oranges are reliably sweet (and they're conveniently seedless), but juicier Valencias would work well in this recipe, too. A cup of cappuccino and a crisp cookie would go well with the oranges.

1 tablespoon slivered orange zest
½ cup sugar
2 tablespoons fresh lemon juice
4 large navel oranges
2 tablespoons sliced almonds, toasted

1. In a medium saucepan, combine the orange zest, sugar, and lemon juice, stirring well to combine. Cook over medium heat, without stirring, until the syrup is pale amber in color, about 5 minutes.

2. Meanwhile, with a paring knife, peel the skin and outer membranes from the oranges. Cut each orange crosswise into five ½-inch-thick rounds. Add the oranges to the hot syrup in the saucepan and gently spoon the sauce over the oranges. Divide the oranges among 4 plates and spoon the sauce and zest over. Serve at room temperature or chilled; sprinkle with the almonds just before serving.

Helpful hint: Be careful when adding the oranges to the pan of hot syrup: Lay the slices gently in the syrup so that it does not splatter.

Fat: 2g/9%
Calories: 196
Saturated Fat: .2g
Carbohydrate: 47g
Protein: 2g
Cholesterol: 0mg
Sodium: 2mg

FRUIT WITH CANNOLI CREAM

SERVES: 4
WORKING TIME: 10 MINUTES
TOTAL TIME: 10 MINUTES

1 cup part-skim ricotta cheese

⅓ cup sugar

¾ teaspoon grated orange zest

3 tablespoons orange juice

2 tablespoons mini chocolate chips

1 apple, cored and cut into 8 wedges

1 pear, cored and cut into 8 wedges

1 plum, pitted and cut into 8 wedges

1 pint strawberries, hulled

1. In a food processor, combine the ricotta, sugar, orange zest, and orange juice and process until smooth. Transfer the mixture to a medium bowl and fold in 1 tablespoon of the chocolate chips.

2. Place the fruit on a platter, spoon the ricotta mixture on the side, sprinkle with the remaining 1 tablespoon chocolate chips, and serve.

Helpful hint: You can also arrange the fruit in four large goblets and top each portion with some of the cream and chocolate chips.

FAT: 7G/25%
CALORIES: 257
SATURATED FAT: 3.9G
CARBOHYDRATE: 44G
PROTEIN: 8G
CHOLESTEROL: 19MG
SODIUM: 78MG

Cannoli are crisp tube-shaped pastries filled with a chocolate-dotted ricotta cream; the cannoli shells are deep-fried before they're filled, making this a dessert to avoid if you're watching your fat intake. But you can still enjoy the flavor of the ricotta cream as a topping for fresh fruit. We've used part-skim ricotta for this slim but luscious treat.

BANANA GRATIN WITH MARSALA CREAM

SERVES: 4
WORKING TIME: 10 MINUTES
TOTAL TIME: 10 MINUTES

*I*n
this delicious dessert,
broiled bananas glazed
with brown sugar are
served over a creamy
sauce flavored with
Marsala.

⅓ cup reduced-fat sour cream

¼ cup plain nonfat yogurt

¼ cup firmly packed light
brown sugar

2 tablespoons Marsala wine

¾ teaspoon grated lemon zest

⅛ teaspoon nutmeg

4 large bananas, peeled and
sliced on the diagonal into
¾-inch long pieces

2 tablespoons fresh lemon juice

1. In a small bowl, combine the sour cream, yogurt, 2 tablespoons of the brown sugar, the Marsala, lemon zest, and nutmeg. Refrigerate until serving time.

2. Preheat the broiler. Arrange the banana pieces in a single layer on a broilerproof pan. Sprinkle the lemon juice over the bananas, then sprinkle with the remaining 2 tablespoons brown sugar. Broil 6 inches from the heat for 4 minutes, or until the sugar has melted and the bananas are heated through. Divide the Marsala cream among 4 plates, top with the bananas, and serve.

Helpful hint: To speed the ripening of bananas, place them in a plastic bag with a slice of apple and store at room temperature or in a slightly warm place.

FAT: 3G/12%
CALORIES: 226
SATURATED FAT: 1.6G
CARBOHYDRATE: 48G
PROTEIN: 4G
CHOLESTEROL; 7MG
SODIUM: 29MG

Brutti ma Buoni

MAKES: 2 DOZEN COOKIES
WORKING TIME: 15 MINUTES
TOTAL TIME: 1 HOUR

⅓ cup hazelnuts
½ cup egg whites (about 4)
¼ teaspoon salt
¼ teaspoon cream of tartar
1 cup sugar
1½ teaspoons Frangelico or
½ teaspoon vanilla extract
2 tablespoons unsweetened
cocoa powder
¼ teaspoon cinnamon
⅛ teaspoon ground cloves

1. Preheat the oven to 375°. Toast the hazelnuts on a baking sheet until the skins begin to flake and the nuts are fragrant, about 7 minutes. Reduce the oven temperature to 275°. Place the nuts in a kitchen towel and rub vigorously to remove their skins (some pieces will remain). When cool enough to handle, coarsely chop the hazelnuts.

2. Line 2 baking sheets with nonstick parchment paper or spray the sheets with nonstick cooking spray and dust with flour. Set aside.

3. In a large bowl, with an electric mixer, beat the egg whites, salt, and cream of tartar until soft peaks form. Gradually beat in the sugar, 1 tablespoon at a time, until the egg whites are very stiff and shiny, about 10 minutes. Beat in the Frangelico.

4. With a rubber spatula, fold in the cocoa powder, cinnamon, and cloves. Gently fold in the hazelnuts. Drop by rounded teaspoonfuls onto the prepared baking sheets. Bake until the cookies are crisp and set, about 30 minutes.

Helpful hint: Frangelico is an Italian liqueur flavored with hazelnuts. Amaretto, an almond-flavored liqueur, could be used instead.

VALUES ARE PER COOKIE
FAT: 1G/20%
CALORIES: 46
SATURATED FAT: .1G
CARBOHYDRATE: 9G
PROTEIN: 1G
CHOLESTEROL: 0MG
SODIUM: 31MG

Modestly named "ugly but good," these feather-light meringue cookies are flavored with cocoa and cinnamon.

PLUMS POACHED IN RED WINE

SERVES: 4
WORKING TIME: 10 MINUTES
TOTAL TIME: 30 MINUTES PLUS CHILLING TIME

Summer fruits poached in spiced wine are a favorite Italian dessert. Instead of a dollop of whipped cream or the super-rich cheese called mascarpone, the fruit here is topped with a creamy mixture of reduced-fat sour cream and nonfat yogurt. This topping would be lovely with other desserts—warm gingerbread, dried-fruit compote, or homemade applesauce, for instance.

⅔ cup plain nonfat yogurt

2 tablespoons reduced-fat sour cream

1 cup dry red wine

⅓ cup sugar

1 vanilla bean, split, or ½ teaspoon vanilla extract

Two 3 x ½-inch strips of orange zest

¼ teaspoon ground ginger

6 red or purple plums, halved and pitted

1. In a small bowl, combine the yogurt and sour cream. Cover and refrigerate until serving time.

2. In a medium saucepan, combine the wine, sugar, vanilla bean (if using the vanilla extract, do not add it now), orange zest, and ginger. Bring to a boil over medium heat, reduce the heat to a simmer, and add the plums, cut-sides down. Cook, turning once, until the plums are tender, about 12 minutes. With a slotted spoon, transfer the plums to a shallow bowl and set aside. Return the syrup to the heat and cook, stirring occasionally, until reduced to ½ cup, about 8 minutes. If using the vanilla extract, stir it into the mixture now.

3. Pour the reduced syrup over the plums and cool to room temperature. Chill the plums in the syrup for at least 1 hour and up to 3 days. To serve, remove the orange zest and vanilla bean. Spoon the plums and syrup into 4 dessert bowls and spoon a dollop of the yogurt cream into the bowl.

Helpful Hint: The vanilla bean can be reused after the plums have cooled: Rinse and dry the bean and place it in the container where you store your sugar to infuse the sugar with a subtle vanilla flavor.

FAT: 2G/12%
CALORIES: 149
SATURATED FAT: .6G
CARBOHYDRATE: 33G
PROTEIN: 3G
CHOLESTEROL: 3MG
SODIUM: 21MG

STRAWBERRIES WITH BALSAMIC VINEGAR

SERVES: 4
WORKING TIME: 10 MINUTES
TOTAL TIME: 20 MINUTES

Just as a squeeze of lime brings out the full flavor of melon, a bit of mild balsamic vinegar does wonderful things for strawberries. The syrup can be cooked the day before serving, but it's best to hull and slice the berries no more than an hour ahead of time. Pour the syrup over the strawberries just 20 to 30 minutes before serving, or the fruit will become mushy.

⅓ cup sugar
Three 3 x ½-inch strips of orange zest
Three 3 x ½-inch strips of lemon zest
3 tablespoons balsamic vinegar
2 pints strawberries, hulled and halved

1. In a small skillet or saucepan, combine the sugar and ¼ cup of water, stirring to blend. Add the orange zest and lemon zest and bring to a boil over medium heat. Boil for 2 minutes, remove from the heat, cover, and let cool to room temperature, about 20 minutes. Remove the orange zest and lemon zest and discard.

2. Transfer the syrup to a medium bowl and stir in the vinegar. Add the strawberries, tossing to coat. Spoon the berries and syrup into 4 bowls and serve.

Helpful hint: Any time you're about to eat an orange or juice a lemon, peel off the zest in wide strips, wrap it, and freeze it. This way, you'll always have citrus zest on hand when you need it.

FAT: 1G/8%
CALORIES: 116
SATURATED FAT: 0G
CARBOHYDRATE: 29G
PROTEIN: 1G
CHOLESTEROL: 0MG
SODIUM: 3MG

Granita *is the lightest of the many Italian frozen desserts: It's a fruit or coffee ice, crunchy with tiny ice crystals created by stirring the mixture as it freezes. Frozen berries are fine for this fruit granita, but you could, of course, use fresh. Or, just buy a small box of fresh berries for garnishing the granita; a mint sprig is another pretty touch.*

RASPBERRY GRANITA

SERVES: 4
WORKING TIME: 10 MINUTES
TOTAL TIME: 10 MINUTES PLUS FREEZING TIME

2 cups dry white wine

Two 12-ounce packages frozen raspberries (not in syrup), thawed

½ cup sugar

1 tablespoon light corn syrup

⅛ teaspoon nutmeg

Two 3 x ½-inch strips of lemon zest

2 tablespoons grenadine syrup

1. In a medium saucepan, combine the wine, raspberries, sugar, corn syrup, nutmeg, and lemon zest. Bring to a boil over medium heat and cook for 1 minute to melt the sugar. Remove from the heat and push through a fine-mesh sieve into a bowl; discard the seeds. Stir in the grenadine syrup.

2. Transfer the mixture to a shallow container large enough so that the granita mixture is no deeper than ½ inch. Freeze until frozen around the edges, about 1 hour. With a fork, pull the solid edges in toward the liquid center until well combined (see tip). Freeze again. To serve, scrape the granita with a spoon or fork and spoon into 4 wineglasses or dessert bowls.

Helpful hint: Grenadine is a concentrated flavoring syrup that was originally made from pomegranates and may now be made from various fruits; it is sold in liquor stores and supermarkets. An equal amount of frozen raspberry or cranberry juice concentrate may be substituted for the grenadine.

TIP

To keep the granita coarsely textured, and to ensure that it freezes evenly, stir it after it's frozen around the edges, but still soft in the middle, bringing the frozen bits from the bottom and sides of the pan toward the center.

FAT: 2G/6%
CALORIES: 303
SATURATED FAT: 0G
CARBOHYDRATE: 58G
PROTEIN: 2G
CHOLESTEROL: 0MG
SODIUM: 12MG

RICOTTA CHEESECAKE

SERVES: 12
WORKING TIME: 20 MINUTES
TOTAL TIME: 1 HOUR

¾ cup graham cracker crumbs

2 teaspoons vegetable oil

¾ cup plus 2 tablespoons sugar

½ cup golden raisins

3 tablespoons Amaretto, Marsala, or brandy

15-ounce container part-skim ricotta cheese

1 cup low-fat (1%) cottage cheese

3 tablespoons flour

2 whole eggs, well beaten

3 egg whites

¾ teaspoon grated orange zest

¾ teaspoon grated lemon zest

¾ teaspoon vanilla extract

2 tablespoons confectioners' sugar

1. Preheat the oven to 375°. Spray a 9-inch deep-dish glass pie plate with nonstick cooking spray. In a small bowl, combine the crumbs, oil, and 2 tablespoons of the sugar. Press the crumb mixture into the bottom and up the sides of the prepared pie plate. Bake for 8 minutes to set the crust. Cool on a wire rack.

2. Meanwhile, in a small bowl, combine the raisins and Amaretto and set aside. In a large bowl, combine the ricotta, cottage cheese, remaining ¾ cup sugar, flour, whole eggs, egg whites, orange zest, lemon zest, and vanilla. Stir in the raisins and Amaretto.

3. Pour the cheese mixture into the prepared crust and bake for 35 minutes. Reduce the oven temperature to 250° and bake for 12 minutes, or until the cheesecake is just set and the edges are slightly brown or a cake tester inserted in the center of the cake comes out clean. Cool slightly and either serve at room temperature or chill and serve cold. Just before serving, dust the top of the cake with the confectioners' sugar.

Helpful hint: You can also make the crust with amaretti (Italian almond-flavored cookies): Crush 12 large amaretti in a food processor (you should have ¾ cup crumbs) and stir together with the oil. Omit the 2 tablespoons of sugar used in the graham cracker crust.

FAT: 5G/22%
CALORIES: 209
SATURATED FAT: 2.2G
CARBOHYDRATE: 31G
PROTEIN: 9G
CHOLESTEROL: 47MG
SODIUM: 191MG

Crostata di ricotta—Italian cheesecake—is baked in a buttery pastry crust, with strips of pastry crisscrossed over the top. By making the cake with a crumb crust instead, we've been able to leave the delicious filling largely unchanged, yet the result is still low in fat. The citrusy ricotta filling is flavored with Amaretto and studded with plump golden raisins.

PEACHES AND CREAM WITH RASPBERRY SAUCE

SERVES: 4
WORKING TIME: 10 MINUTES
TOTAL TIME: 10 MINUTES

Richly colored like a Renaissance tapestry, this dish poses sweet summer fruits on a "painted" backdrop. Be sure the peaches are at peak flavor and texture as well as picture perfect: The best time to try this dessert would be when locally grown peaches are plentiful.

12-ounce package frozen (not in syrup) raspberries, thawed
¼ cup honey
¼ cup plain nonfat yogurt
2 tablespoons reduced-fat sour cream
½ teaspoon vanilla extract
4 large peaches, halved and pitted
½ cup fresh raspberries

1. In a food processor, combine the frozen raspberries and honey and process to a purée. Strain the mixture through a fine-mesh sieve into a bowl; discard the seeds.

2. In a medium bowl, combine the yogurt, sour cream, and vanilla. Reserving ¼ cup of the raspberry purée, divide the remainder among 4 dessert bowls. Dividing evenly, place 2 or 3 dollops of the sour cream mixture on top of the raspberry purée and with a sharp knife, briefly swirl the sour cream mixture into a decorative pattern.

3. Place the peaches in the bowls. Top with the fresh raspberries and spoon the reserved raspberry purée on top. Serve immediately or chill for later.

Helpful hints: Choose peaches with a creamy-yellow background color: Whether or not there's a red blush depends on the variety, not the stage of ripeness. Don't buy rock-hard fruit—check for a slight softness at the peach's "seam." Store firm peaches in a paper bag at room temperature for a few days; they will soften and become more fragrant, but not sweeter.

FAT: 2G/9%
CALORIES: 211
SATURATED FAT: .5G
CARBOHYDRATE: 51G
PROTEIN: 4G
CHOLESTEROL: 3MG
SODIUM: 16MG

ESPRESSO SEMIFREDDO

SERVES: 4
WORKING TIME: 10 MINUTES
TOTAL TIME: 20 MINUTES PLUS FREEZING TIME

As the name suggests, a semifreddo—a sort of frozen mousse—is only "half frozen." Heavy cream and eggs are the basis for a traditional semifreddo, but we've taken a lighter route with this coffee-flavored dessert, using low-fat milk, part-skim ricotta, and just one egg yolk (egg whites contain no fat). A banana adds creamy richness, as well.

2 cups low-fat (1%) milk
⅓ cup firmly packed light brown sugar
1 whole egg
2 egg whites
2 tablespoons instant espresso powder
¾ cup part-skim ricotta cheese
1 banana, cut into 3 or 4 pieces
2 tablespoons Frangelico or Amaretto
2 tablespoons plus 2 teaspoons chocolate syrup

1. In a medium saucepan, combine the milk and sugar and bring to a simmer over medium heat. Remove from the heat.

2. In a medium bowl, combine the whole egg and egg whites, whisking well. Gradually whisk a little of the hot milk mixture into the egg mixture. Stir the warmed eggs into the saucepan, return it to medium heat, and cook, stirring constantly, until the custard thickens enough to coat the back of a spoon, about 10 minutes. Add the espresso powder, stirring to combine.

3. Transfer the custard to a food processor. Add the ricotta, banana, and Frangelico and purée until smooth. Line an 8½ x 4½-inch loaf pan with plastic wrap, leaving a 4-inch overhang. Transfer the mixture to the prepared loaf pan and freeze until mostly frozen, but still easy to slice, about 4 hours. To unmold, run a small metal spatula between the plastic wrap and the sides of the pan to loosen the loaf. Invert the pan onto a platter or cutting board and remove the pan and the plastic wrap. Dip a long knife into hot water and slice the loaf into 8 even slices. Divide among 4 plates, drizzle with the chocolate syrup, and serve.

Helpful hint: Instant espresso is sold in many supermarkets (it comes in jars). If you substitute regular instant coffee, be sure to use powdered, not granular or freeze-dried, which will not dissolve as well.

FAT: 6G/19%
CALORIES: 288
SATURATED FAT: 3.6G
CARBOHYDRATE: 43G
PROTEIN: 13G
CHOLESTEROL: 72MG
SODIUM: 182MG

GLOSSARY

Amaretti—Crisp Italian macaroons made from egg whites, sugar, and apricot kernels, which have an intense almond-like flavor. Amaretti are low in fat, making them a good ingredient for Italian desserts. Look for them at gourmet shops and Italian grocery stores.

Anchovies/Anchovy paste—Tiny preserved fish and the convenient condiment made from them. Whole anchovy fillets, salt-cured or oil-packed, should be rinsed and patted dry before using to remove some of the salt or oil. Anchovy paste, which is sold in tubes, is made by mashing the fish with vinegar, spices, and water. Used in small amounts, anchovies in either form contribute robust flavor and only minimal fat.

Artichoke—The bud of a thistle-like plant, this delicious vegetable is extremely popular in Italy. The bases of the leaves and the fleshy bottom, or heart, of the artichoke are edible; the tough parts of the leaves and the fuzzy interior "choke" are discarded. Select heavy artichokes with tight leaves and fresh-looking stems; refrigerate them in a plastic bag for no longer than three to four days.

Basil—A highly fragrant herb with a flavor somewhere between licorice and cloves. Like many fresh herbs, basil will retain more of its taste if added at the end of cooking; dried basil is milder, but can still be used to advantage in soups and stews. Fresh basil, widely available in the summer, is indispensable for making pesto, the intensely flavorful Italian pasta sauce. To store, refrigerate, unwashed, in a jar of water, covered with a plastic bag, for up to three days.

Beans, cannellini—Large white kidney beans often used in Italian cooking. Cannellini are sold both dried and canned. Like all canned beans, cannellini should be rinsed and drained before use; this removes much of the sodium present in the canning liquid and also gives the beans a fresher flavor. Look for cannellini in the canned vegetable or Italian foods section of your supermarket.

Beans, Italian green—Broad, flat green beans; sometimes called Romano beans. Italian green beans are widely available frozen; they add an authentic touch to Italian meals. Be sure not to overcook the frozen beans, as they should retain their bright green color.

Capers—The flower buds of a small bush found in Mediterranean countries. To make capers, the buds are dried and then pickled in vinegar with some salt: To reduce saltiness, rinse before using. The piquant taste of capers permeates any sauce quickly, and just a few supply a big flavor boost.

Clam juice, bottled—A convenient form of clam juice. It adds a briny flavor to seafood sauces, soups, and chowders. If using canned clams or oysters rather than fresh, the addition of bottled clam juice intensifies the seafood flavor. If clam juice is unavailable, you can substitute chicken broth.

Cocoa powder, unsweetened—Pure chocolate from which most of the cocoa butter has been pressed. Cocoa is a boon to low-fat dessert making since it is low in fat when compared with solid chocolate. "Dutch-process" cocoa is treated with alkali, which neutralizes some of the acid in the cocoa, giving it a less harsh flavor.

Cream cheese, reduced fat—A light cream cheese, commonly called Neufchâtel, with about one-third less fat than regular cream cheese. It can be used as a substitute for regular cream cheese. A small amount used in baking or in sauces duplicates the richness of full-fat cheese or heavy cream.

Eggplant—An oval-, pear-, or zucchini-shaped vegetable with purple or white skin and porous pale-green flesh. Eggplant is very popular in Italy, where it is often baked, fried, or stuffed. Since the spongy flesh readily soaks up oil, it's better to bake, broil, or grill eggplant; the last two methods give this vegetable a deep, smoky flavor as well. Choose a firm, glossy, unblemished eggplant that seems heavy for its size. Don't buy eggplant too far in advance—it will turn bitter if kept too long. Store eggplant in the refrigerator for three to four days.

Fennel, fresh—A vegetable resembling a head of celery in shape and texture, with a subtle licorice flavor. The feathery fronds that top the stalks are used as an herb, and the bulb is used raw in salads, or cooked in sauces; its flavor complements fish particularly well. Fresh fennel is an Italian favorite and is often found in Italian markets, where it may be called *finocchio*. Choose firm, unblemished fennel bulbs with fresh green fronds. Store in the refrigerator in a plastic bag for three to four days.

Fennel seeds—The seeds of the common fennel plant, which have a slightly sweet, licorice-like taste. Fennel seeds are often used to season Italian sausages, and are also used in pasta sauces and with seafood.

Garlic—The edible bulb of a plant closely related to onions, leeks, and chives. One of the seasonings most associated with Italian cuisine, garlic can be pungently assertive or sweetly mild, depending on how it is prepared: Minced or crushed garlic yields a more powerful flavor than whole or halved cloves. Whereas sautéing turns garlic rich and savory, slow mmering or roasting produces a mild, mellow flavor. Select rm, plump heads with dry skins; avoid heads that have egun to sprout. Store garlic in an open or loosely covered ontainer in a cool, dark place for up to 2 months.

Gorgonzola cheese —An Italian blue cheese made from ow's milk. Young Gorgonzola is fairly mild and then ecomes stronger with age. This cheese is often used to flavor olenta or pasta sauces.

Hazelnuts Sweet, richly flavored nuts, also called filberts. Hazelnuts are used in Italian cakes, cookies, nougats, and chocolates. Refrigerate shelled hazelnuts for up to six months. To remove the papery brown skins, toast the hazelnuts in a 350° oven for five to seven minutes; then rub off the skins with a kitchen towel.

Honey—A liquid sweetener made by honeybees from flower nectar. It ranges in flavor from mild (orange blossom) to very strong (buckwheat). Deliciously versatile, honey can sweeten savory sauces or fruit desserts. Store honey at room temperature. If it crystallizes, place the open jar in a pan of warm water for a few minutes; or microwave it for 15 seconds, or until the honey liquifies.

Lemon juice—Fresh lemon juice is used in Italian cooking to cut the richness of sautéed veal, to accent the flavor of seafood, and to bring out the sweetness of fresh fruit; bottled lemon juice is a poor substitute. Halve lemons crosswise and squeeze them by hand, use a citrus juicer or lemon reamer, or try an inexpensive lemon spigot, which is inserted in the fruit and lets you pour the juice out as if through a faucet.

Mozzarella cheese—A very mild-flavored Italian cheese with exceptional melting properties. Mozzarella was originally made from water-buffalo milk, but is now more commonly made from cow's milk; it is available in whole milk, part-skim, and fat-free varieties. The part-skim variety is the best option for cooking, as it is relatively low in fat but still has a nice texture and good melting properties. The rubbery texture of nonfat mozzarella makes it unsuitable for most recipes.

Olive oil—A fragrant oil pressed from olives. Olive oil is one of the signature ingredients of Italian cuisine. This oil is rich in monounsaturated fats, which make it more healthful than butter and other solid shortenings. Olive oil comes in different grades, reflecting the method used to refine the oil and the resulting level of acidity. The finest, most expensive oil is cold-pressed extra-virgin, which should be reserved for flavoring salad dressings and other uncooked or lightly cooked foods. Virgin and pure olive oils are slightly more acidic with less olive flavor, and are fine for most types of cooking.

Olives—Small, oval fruits native to the Mediterranean region with an intense, earthy taste. Olives are picked green (unripe) or black (ripe) and then must be cured—in oil or brine—to mellow their natural bitterness and develop their flavor; herbs and other seasonings are added to create a wide variety of olives. The Calamata, a purple-black, brine-cured olive, is widely available; although it's a Greek-style olive, the Calamata is a good choice for pasta sauces and other Italian dishes. You may find quality Italian olives, such as Gaetas, in Italian delis and grocery stores. Use all olives sparingly since they are high in fat (olive oil).

Parmesan cheese—An intensely flavored, hard grating cheese. Genuine Italian Parmesan, stamped "Parmigiano-Reggiano" on the rind, is produced in the Emilia-Romagna region, and tastes richly nutty with a slight sweetness. For a fine, fluffy texture that melts into hot foods, grate the cheese in a hand-cranked grater. Buy Parmesan in blocks and grate it as needed for best flavor and freshness.

Parsley—A popular herb available in two varieties. Curly parsley, with lacy, frilly leaves, is quite mild and is preferred for garnishing, while flat-leaf Italian parsley has a stronger flavor and is better for cooking. Store parsley as you would basil. Since fresh parsley is so widely available, there is really no reason to use dried, which has very little flavor.

Peppers, bell—The large, sweet members of the *Capsicum* family of vegetables. Green bell peppers are most common; red peppers have ripened and are sweeter. You can also buy yellow, orange, purple and brown bell peppers in some markets. Choose well-colored, firm peppers that are heavy for their size; these will have thick, juicy flesh. Store peppers in a plastic bag in the refrigerator for up to a week. Before preparing bell peppers, remove the stem, spongy ribs, and seeds.

Pine nuts—The seeds of certain pine trees that grow in several parts of the world, including Italy. Called *pignoli* or *pinoli* in Italian, they are best known for their role in pesto, the classic basil sauce for pasta; they're also used in cookies and other desserts. Use pine nuts sparingly, since they are high in fat. Look for them in the Italian foods section of your market. Store the nuts in a tightly closed jar in the freezer for up to six months. Toast pine nuts briefly before using to bring out their full flavor.

Prosciutto—A salt-cured, air-dried Italian ham that originated in the area around the city of Parma. This dense-textured, intensely flavored ham is served as an appetizer with melon or figs and also used in cooking, often to flavor sauces. Prosciutto has been produced in the United States for years, but imported Italian prosciutto is also available; the finest is labeled "Prosciutto de Parma." Our recipes should be made with very thinly sliced *prosciutto crudo* (raw) rather than *prosciutto cotto* (cooked).

Rice, arborio—A *superfino* variety from Italy's Po Valley. Arborio is the preferred rice for risotto, because the grain aborbs much more liquid than other rices; its starchy exterior becomes creamy while the center remains slightly firm. Arborio is sold in some supermarkets and in gourmet and Italian food shops.

Ricotta cheese—A fresh, creamy white, Italian cheese with a grainier texture than cottage cheese and a slightly sweet flavor. Available in whole-milk and part-skim versions, it is often used in stuffed and baked pastas, and a little part-skim ricotta can be stirred into a sauce for added richness as well as creamy body.

Romano cheese—A hard grating cheese similar to Parmesan but with a saltier, more robust flavor. Italian Romano cheese is traditionally made from sheep's milk and is called *pecorino Romano;* the American version is most often made from cow's milk (or a blend of cow's and goat's or sheep's milk). Grate Romano as you would Parmesan and use it in assertively flavored dishes; Romano can overpower more delicate foods.

Rosemary—An aromatic herb with needle-like leaves and a sharp pine-citrus flavor. Italians often season roasts—poultry, beef, lamb, or pork—with rosemary. If you can't get fresh rosemary, use whole dried leaves, which retain the flavor of the fresh herb quite well. Crush or chop rosemary leaves with a mortar and pestle or a chef's knife.

Sage—An intensely fragrant herb with grayish-green leaves. An Italian favorite, especially for roasted meat and poultry, sage will infuse a dish with a pleasant, musty mint taste. In its dried form, sage is sold as whole leaves, ground, and in a fluffy "rubbed" version.

Sour cream—A soured dairy product, resulting from treating sweet cream with a lactic acid culture. It can be used in savory dishes and may also be used as a dessert topping, where it offers a tart counterpoint to the sweetnes. Regular sour cream contains at least 18 percent milk fat by volume; reduced-fat sour cream contains 4 percent fat; nonfat sour cream is, of course, fat-free. In cooking, the reduced-fat version can be substituted for regular sour cream; use the nonfat cautiously since it behaves differently, especially in baking.

Spinach, fresh and frozen—A nutrient-rich, dark-green, leafy vegetable. Fresh spinach has crisp, emerald green leaves; it will keep its bright color if not overcooked. Frozen spinach, a convenient substitute, can be used when the spinach will be chopped or puréed. When buying fresh spinach, choose springy, green bunches; avoid withered or yellowing leaves. Wash spinach carefully, as it is often gritty: Submerge the leaves in a large bowl of water, swirl them with your hands, then lift out the leaves. Even bagged spinach labeled "pre-washed" should be rinsed.

Squash, butternut—A large, lightbulb-shaped winter squash. This firm-fleshed, starchy vegetable can be baked, boiled, or steamed. Northern Italians often cook with pumpkin, for which butternut squash makes a fine stand-in. Pick an unbruised squash with no dark or soft spots and store it in a cool place for up to a month. Use a large, heavy knife to cut the squash; it can be peeled either before or after cooking.

Tomato paste—A concentrated essence of cooked tomatoes, sold in cans and tubes. This Italian ingredient is commonly used to thicken and accent the flavor and color of sauces; however, it is slightly bitter and should not be used alone or in large quantities. If you're using only part of a can of tomato paste, save the remainder by freezing it in a plastic bag.

Tomatoes, fresh—Juicy red fruit-vegetables that are a staple of Italian cuisine. There are several types to choose from: Meaty beefsteak tomatoes, globe tomatoes (best for slicing), and egg-shaped plum tomatoes, which tend to be fleshier and less juicy than the other two types. Smaller cherry and pear tomatoes are great for salads and garnishes, and may also be cooked. The best tomatoes are the locally grown ones you buy in season. Cold destroys both the flavor and texture of tomatoes, so never refrigerate them. When ripe tomatoes are unavailable, consider substituting good-quality canned tomatoes, which will work perfectly in many recipes. A 16-ounce can of peeled tomatoes yields one cup, drained.

Vanilla bean—The dried pod of a climbing orchid. A whole vanilla bean can be simmered in liquids such as milk for custards, or the pod can be split and the seeds scraped into a batter or other mixture. To reuse the bean after cooking, rinse, blot dry, and store in a sugar canister, where it will also impart a vanilla flavor to the sugar. Pure vanilla extract is a convenient substitute, but avoid imitation vanilla, which has a bitter, chemical aftertaste.

Zest, citrus—The thin, outermost colored part of the rind of citrus fruits that contains strongly flavored oils. Zest imparts a unique, intense flavor that helps to compensate for a lack of fat. Remove zest with a grater, zester, or vegetable peeler.

Index

TIME LIFE BOOKS

Time-Life Books is a division of Time Life Inc.

PRESIDENT and CEO: John M. Fahey Jr.

TIME-LIFE BOOKS

MANAGING EDITOR: Roberta Conlan

Director of Design: Michael Hentges
Editorial Production Manager: Ellen Robling
Senior Editors: Russell B. Adams Jr., Janet Cave, Lee Hassig,
   Robert Somerville, Henry Woodhead
Special Projects Editor: Rita Thievon Mullin
Director of Operations: Eileen Bradley
Director of Photography and Research: John Conrad Weiser
Library: Louise D. Forstall

PRESIDENT: John D. Hall

Vice President, Director of New Product Development: Neil Kagan
Associate Director, New Product Development: Quentin S. McAndrew
Marketing Director, New Product Development: Robin B. Shuster
Vice President, Book Production: Marjann Caldwell
Production Manager: Marlene Zack
Consulting Editor: Catherine Boland Hackett

Design for Great Taste-Low Fat by David Fridberg of
Miles Fridberg Molinaroli, Inc.

REBUS, INC.

PUBLISHER: Rodney M. Friedman
EDITORIAL DIRECTOR: Charles L. Mee

Editorial Staff for *Italian Cooking*
Director, Recipe Development and Photography: Grace Young
Editorial Director: Kate Slate
Senior Recipe Developer: Sandra Rose Gluck
Recipe Developers: Helen Jones, Paul Piccuito
Writer: Bonnie J. Slotnick
Associate Editor: Julee Binder Shapiro
Editorial Assistant: James W. Brown, Jr
Nutritionists: Hill Nutrition Associates

Art Director: Timothy Jeffs
Photographer: Lisa Koenig
Photographer's Assistants: Katie Everard, Rainer Fehringer,
   Robert Presciutti
Food Stylists: A.J. Battifarano, Karen Pickus, Roberta Rall, Karen Tack
Assistant Food Stylists: Mako Antonishek, Catherine Chatham,
   Amy Lord, Ellie Ritt
Prop Stylist: Debrah Donahue
Prop Coordinator: Karin Martin

Library of Congress Cataloging-in-Publication Data

Italian cooking.
  p.   cm. -- (Great taste, low fat)
Includes index.
ISBN 0-7835-4557-6
1. Cookery, Italian. 2. Low-fat diet--Recipes. 3. Quick and easy
cookery. I. Time-Life Books. II. Series.
TX723.I813   1996
641.5945--dc20   95-48207
                                                      CIP

Other Publications
THE TIME-LIFE COMPLETE GARDENER
HOME REPAIR AND IMPROVEMENT
JOURNEY THROUGH THE MIND AND BODY
WEIGHT WATCHERS® SMART CHOICE RECIPE COLLECTION
TRUE CRIME
THE AMERICAN INDIANS
THE ART OF WOODWORKING
LOST CIVILIZATIONS
ECHOES OF GLORY
THE NEW FACE OF WAR
HOW THINGS WORK
WINGS OF WAR
CREATIVE EVERYDAY COOKING
COLLECTOR'S LIBRARY OF THE UNKNOWN
CLASSICS OF WORLD WAR II
TIME-LIFE LIBRARY OF CURIOUS AND UNUSUAL FACTS
VOYAGE THROUGH THE UNIVERSE
THE THIRD REICH
MYSTERIES OF THE UNKNOWN
TIME FRAME
FIX IT YOURSELF
FITNESS, HEALTH & NUTRITION
SUCCESSFUL PARENTING
HEALTHY HOME COOKING
UNDERSTANDING COMPUTERS
LIBRARY OF NATIONS
THE ENCHANTED WORLD
THE KODAK LIBRARY OF CREATIVE PHOTOGRAPHY
GREAT MEALS IN MINUTES
THE CIVIL WAR
PLANET EARTH
THE EPIC OF FLIGHT
THE GOOD COOK
WORLD WAR II
THE OLD WEST

*For information on and a full description of any of the Time-Life Books series
listed above, please call 1-800-621-7026 or write:*
Reader Information
Time-Life Customer Service
P.O. Box C-32068
Richmond, Virginia 23261-2068

METRIC CONVERSION CHARTS

VOLUME EQUIVALENTS
(fluid ounces/milliliters and liters)

US	Metric
1 tsp	5 ml
1 tbsp (½ fl oz)	15 ml
¼ cup (2 fl oz)	60 ml
⅓ cup	80 ml
½ cup (4 fl oz)	120 ml
⅔ cup	160 ml
¾ cup (6 fl oz)	180 ml
1 cup (8 fl oz)	240 ml
1 qt (32 fl oz)	950 ml
1 qt + 3 tbsps	1 L
1 gal (128 fl oz)	4 L

Conversion formula
Fluid ounces X 30 = milliliters
1000 milliliters = 1 liter

WEIGHT EQUIVALENTS
(ounces and pounds/grams and kilograms)

US	Metric
¼ oz	7 g
½ oz	15 g
¾ oz	20 g
1 oz	30 g
8 oz (½ lb)	225 g
12 oz (¾ lb)	340 g
16 oz (1 lb)	455 g
35 oz (2.2 lbs)	1 kg

Conversion formula
Ounces X 28.35 = grams
1000 grams = 1 kilogram

LINEAR EQUIVALENTS
(inches and feet/centimeters and meters)

US	Metric
¼ in	.75 cm
½ in	1.5 cm
¾ in	2 cm
1 in	2.5 cm
6 in	15 cm
12 in (1 ft)	30 cm
39 in	1 m

Conversion formula
Inches X 2.54 = centimeters
100 centimeters = 1 meter

TEMPERATURE EQUIVALENTS
(Fahrenheit/Celsius)

US	Metric
0° (freezer temperature)	-18°
32° (water freezes)	0°
98.6°	37°
180° (water simmers*)	82°
212° (water boils*)	100°
250° (low oven)	120°
350° (moderate oven)	175°
425° (hot oven)	220°
500° (very hot oven)	260°

*at sea level

Conversion formula
Degrees Fahrenheit minus
32 ÷ 1.8 = degrees Celsius